Echoes
of the
Soul

Echoes of the Soul

The Soul's Journey Beyond the Light Through Life, Death, and Life After Death

Echo L. Bodine

NEW WORLD LIBRARY
Novato, California

New World Library
14 Pamaron Way
Novato, California 94949

Library of Congress Cataloging-in-Publication Data
Echoes of the soul: / by Echo L. Bodine.
        p. cm.
"The soul's journey beyond the light through life, death,
and life after death."
Includes bibliographical references.
ISBN 1-57731-076-4 (alk. paper)
    1. Soul.   2. Spiritualism.   I. Title.
        BF1275.S55B63   1999
133.9--dc21   98-42956
                                                CIP

First Printing, February 1999
ISBN 1-57731-076-4
Printed in the Canada on acid-free paper
Distributed to the trade by Publishers Group West

10 9 8

I would like to dedicate this book to my mom,
Mary Opal Mae McKee Bodine.

There is no way I could have written this
book without your *constant* support.
You've really held the vision of this
book for a long time, and I can't thank
you enough for continually
encouraging me to write what I've come
to know as *truth*. I am truly blessed to
have you as my mom. Thanks
for everything.

I love you.

Table of Contents

Acknowledgments

To God, for pushing me on my path so I would keep searching for more and more truth. For my gifts, for Your patience, and for Your continued guidance in my life.

To my very cool family, the Bodines! We've been through so much this lifetime that it sometimes boggles my mind; yet, we just keep growing and getting better. Thanks for everything. I love you.

To my son, Kurt, for all our great talks, for helping me with the research, for believing in the book, and especially for believing in me. I love you, baby.

To my editor, Sheryl Grassie, for your vision with this wonderful book and all your help in pulling it together. To Richard, that wonderful husband of yours, for all his feedback and never-ending support. You two are a great team!

To a very special policeman, who chooses to remain anonymous, for trusting me enough to give me the photographs of the soul.

To my wonderful partner, Mike Hartley. Where do I start? All the emotional support? The late-night gab sessions? The constant encouragement? My sounding board twenty-four hours a day? Our "mainstream-New Age" bantering? It's hard to know where to start. Thank you for all you've given me while I worked on this project. You are truly a gift from God. Thanks, honey, for all of it. I love you.

To Dr. Marcie New for all the work on my body, mind, and soul, and for always believing in me and my work.

To Nick Bunick for writing the foreword, for bringing us your wonderful book, *The Messengers,* and for coming into my life at a perfect time. I dearly treasure your friendship.

To my wonderful publisher, Marc Allen, for all your excitement about this project and for all your great phone calls. You are such a delightful person. I feel very blessed to be one of your authors.

To Rev. Ken Williamson, for coming into my life at the perfect time and showing me through your example how to go that extra mile. You are truly a blessing in my life.

To my two buddies, Tom Linzsmeier and Jim Hanson. You've been so supportive in many ways, and I thank you both from the bottom of my heart.

To my sister-in-law, Jamie Sherman, for your great faxes of encouragement, for all your support, and for hanging in there with me every month!

To Sam DiPaola for the use of your poems.

To all my clients who have taught me about the soul.

To all my students for asking your questions.

A special thanks to these special friends: Fran Lindstrom, Warren Anger, Kathy Grove, Ginny Miller, Valerie Celene, Teri Trombley, J. Marie Fieger, Darlene Kvist, Sarah Wilson, The Breakfast Club — Debbie, Sue, and Roberta — and to my lifelong friend, Roman Sherman.

Foreword

As we go through the journey of our life, there are many times that we have questions that we pray to have answered, questions that deal with the very essence of who we are. Is there truly a spiritual world, or is it the creation of poets and mystics? If there is a spiritual world, what is our relationship to that other dimension? Are we mortals, whose existence is confined to our earth experience, or are we souls that God has granted immortality and eternal life?

For over 1,600 years religious teachers have tried to persuade us that we only have one life to live, that salvation and redemption can only be achieved through their churches and that there is a punishing God who will condemn your soul to eternal suffering if you do not abide by the dogmas and doctrines that they are preaching to us. But a spiritual consciousness is spreading throughout the world today. More and more people are recognizing that their minds are the gateway to their hearts and souls, and they are now opening the gates to allow information to come into the hearts and souls that five years ago would not have been available.

More than ever before in history, people are trying to understand their relationship with God. Are we human beings, who coincidentally have a soul? Or are we souls that are having a human experience? There are some individuals who are born with a special gift. For some, the gift may enable them to be an extraordinary singer or a dancer, or a world renowned artist. Or the gift may be of a spiritual nature, in that God has blessed that individual with the ability to not only understand, but also to be able to see into that other dimension, that dimension where God, Jesus, and all the great avatars reside as well as our angels, who are our spiritual guides; into the dimension where the spirits of our loved ones who have passed on have made the transition before us. Echo Bodine is one of those individuals that God has blessed.

I met Echo when I was traveling on a twenty-seven city tour giving spiritual symposiums after my book, *The Messengers,* had been introduced. In Minneapolis, the sponsor and producer of my symposium told me that there was a very special person he wanted to introduce me to, a person that God had given special gifts. I could feel her energy and her spiritual strength.

When she gave me a copy of her manuscript, *Echoes of the Soul,* I read it in two sittings. It had met every criteria that I had established for myself and in other books that I read, in that it was written with love, clarity, and with the intent of helping people to understand their purpose in life and to enjoy the journey that they are on. In *Echoes of the Soul,* you will literally feel that you are sitting in a wonderful, peaceful space and having a personal conversation with Echo Bodine. It is as if one of your best friends is sitting across from you, and in a gentle, loving, conversational manner, is sharing with you her experiences and her insights. And you do not want the conversation to end. Not only does the information being shared with you make sense intellectually, but even more important, your heart and soul will ring with truth, as you come to have a greater understanding of the journey you are on and the true purpose of your life. You will travel with Echo into the spiritual world, and your hearts will be filled with hope and joy, when you truly recognize that there is no such thing as death, but only transitions. You will have both an understanding and a wisdom of the purpose of your life, in that we are all truly on the same journey.

Echoes of the Soul will ease the pain in your own hearts that you experience when you lose a loved one. You will recognize that your loved one and you are only temporarily separated from the material world, but not in the spiritual sense, and that the life that you are living is just one chapter of a magnificent book. Echo Bodine shares her gift with you, just as surely you will share this same gift with others once you have opened the package and witnessed the beauty to the truth and hope that is found within.

Your own soul will echo with joy and peace from the wisdom that is being shared with you. God bless you as you continue on your journey.

— Nick Bunick
Author of *In God's Truth*

The Recovery

The moment I awoke I knew the darkness had ended.
The anesthesia had finally worn off and nothing was
ever going to stop me from remembering.

Who I was, places I've been, lives I've lived, all began
to unfold, layer by layer, just as the rising sun slowly
burns off a cool morning fog. There was a slight feeling
of discomfort, suddenly realizing the truth, but the
clarity made it tolerable. A new form of nakedness
enveloped my body and I was fully aware of every minute
cell making up my existence. Never had I felt so complete.

Problems ceased to have relevance. I now viewed all past
lives as learning experiences, specially designed to get
my soul to this specific point (dare I say) in time.
The process had taken an eternity, yet I feel that it all
took place over the course of one night. Now I understand
how God created the world in seven days.

Yes, creation and consciousness really did explode into
being. Doubt it and you'll continue living in darkness.
Wake up and the fun will truly begin. Never ending.

— Sam DiPaola

Introduction

I was seventeen years old when I discovered that I was born with psychic abilities and the gift of healing, and it took me completely by surprise. Nothing in my mainstream midwestern upbringing, except maybe the voice I heard throughout my childhood, indicated that I or the other members of my family had paranormal abilities.

It all started one night in the fall of 1965 when one of my brothers, who was in the beginning stages of learning to play the drums, went down to the den to practice. My parents, my sister, my other brother, and I had just finished dinner and were still sitting around the table.

My brother played his amateurish best for about five minutes. Then suddenly the clanking noise stopped and beautiful music came from the den. We all looked at Dad, thinking he could somehow explain. But Dad said it must be the Sandy Nelson record he had bought my brother, although we could tell that Dad wasn't convinced, either.

Then the music stopped and my very frightened brother ran up the stairs, hysterically trying to explain what just happened: He was sitting at his drum set with his eyes closed practicing a piece, when a white figure floated through the door and over to him. This figure rested his hands on top of my brother's and began to play the beautiful music we just heard. My brother was so frightened that he had difficulty talking, but he managed to say that even though his eyes were closed the whole time, he could easily see the figure. Then the spirit — or whatever it was — let go of his hands and floated across the room and out the door!

We were stunned. We knew nothing about the occult, as it was called back then. We'd never given much thought to ghosts, spirit guides, or guardian angels other than being taught at an early age that we all have an angel that watches over us. Nothing in our Presbyterian training had prepared us for what just occurred. We sat there not knowing what to say, yet we were filled with questions. We knew my brother would never make up such a story, and we'd just heard the music, so what did it all mean? Why was this happening to my brother? Would the white figure appear to the rest of us?

Mom belonged to a prayer group, and a woman in her group had been to a medium. She called the woman, hoping she could shed some light on what had happened, but she gave Mom the medium's phone number instead. Mom called her right away. Without hesitation the medium told Mom she had been expecting her phone call. She explained that the white figure was my brother's spirit guide who was trying to make himself known. She said that when the guide was living on earth he was a drummer, among many other things, and that he was going to be a teacher for my brother. She also told Mom that

Mom and her four children were all psychically gifted and that she wanted to see us soon for readings.

This information didn't give any of us much peace of mind. A spirit guide that played the drums? We were all gifted? What did *gifted* mean? I asked Mom to make an appointment so that we could find out what it all meant, and a week later I was sitting in Eve Olson's reading room, about to have another life-changing experience.

Eve Olson was a very sweet woman in her fifties who had moved to St. Paul, Minnesota, from England. She had a diploma on the wall from a college in Indiana, and her degree was in mediumship. I had never thought about where people got their psychic abilities, and I was surprised there was actually a college where people could develop that sort of thing. She started my reading by telling me that I was born with the psychic abilities of clairvoyance — the gift of seeing visions, images, or pictures — and also of clairaudience, the gift of hearing spirits. She also said that I was born with the gift of spiritual healing and that I would write books, be on radio and television, travel, and be known throughout the world. As I became older and learned how to work with my abilities, I would then teach others how to develop their psychic and healing gifts.

I told her that I didn't think I had any of these abilities and that I just wanted to have a normal life with a husband and children. She said that ever since I was a little girl I have been able to sense other people's feelings, and it came so naturally to me that I had become used to it and didn't think it was anything special or unusual. She said the reason why I was having so many health problems was because I was very sensitive and didn't know what to do with all the feelings I was always having. My path would be very different from what I had imagined, but this was what my soul wanted for this lifetime. I found this very curious — I had never thought in terms of what my soul wanted.

Eve told Mom that she was also very gifted and that someday she would be a well-known psychic doing readings for people fulltime. She said that my sister, Nikki, wouldn't develop her psychic and healing gifts until she was in her forties, that my brother Michael would be a professional psychic, and that my other brother, whose drumming had started all this inquiry, would choose not to use his abilities. It's been thirty-three years since we first saw Eve — and everything she predicted that night has come true.

Before my session ended, Eve told me to go home and place white hankies on my father's head. She knew he was in bed with a migraine, even though neither Mom nor I had mentioned anything about it. She said to ask God to work through me and to channel healing energy to my father. She said that then I would know what she was talking about.

During our drive home I asked Mom, "Why me? Why do I have these weird gifts? Why can't I have a normal life? What's happening to us? What does all of this mean?"

When we arrived home, I told Dad what the medium had said and asked if I could give this "spiritual healing" a try. He said he was willing, as long as I didn't hurt his head. I neatly laid two hankies on top of his head, placed my hands on top of them, and in a none-too-confident voice asked God to please work through me. Within seconds my hands warmed like heating pads and I could feel energy coming through them. My hands trembled from the energy for a bit, and then after about five minutes they cooled. I slowly took my hands off Dad's head — and he said that his headache was gone!

I didn't sleep at all that night. I lay in bed with an endless stream of questions floating through my head. Should I quit high school and travel around the world healing sick people? Was I responsible for healing all the sick people in the world? Did this mean I was special? Why had God chosen me? Should I join Vista — the domestic Peace Corps? What would my friends say? I wondered if my parents had really named me after a friend of theirs or if they had known there was something different about me and that was why they had given me such an unusual name. How would I become internationally known? How would I overcome my shyness? How do people write books? How would all of this happen? Should I go to church more? Read the Bible more? What about college? I thought back to the male voice I had heard throughout my childhood that would reassure me in times of fear or worry. I wondered if this was why the voice had always told me to go to Sunday school and learn all about Jesus because Jesus was my older brother and had come to earth to show us how to live our lives. As I lay there, I tried to make sense of everything the medium had said. Little did I know it would take years to understand all of it.

Shortly after our first session with Eve, Mom and I began taking psychic development classes from Birdie, a Spiritualist minister in Minneapolis. She was a gifted psychic as well as a tough teacher, which is exactly what I needed. She had the tenacity to stay with me through all my skepticism and endless questions. I wasn't trying to drive her crazy, but all that she was teaching us — astral projection, reincarnation, spirit guides, angels, auras, dowsing, life after death, *plus* psychic development — was rapidly challenging and changing my reality, and I fought it every step of the way. I didn't want my reality to be different from my friends'. I wanted to fit in with everybody else.

Birdie understood what both Mom and I were going through, having been there herself, so she hung in there for a couple of years, presenting new ideas and beliefs to us week after week and helping us develop our psychic abilities. We practiced on friends. It was fun at times and scary at other times — fun to predict good news and scary when I saw difficult or challenging things that were to come.

Part of our psychic development was getting to know our spirit guides, and that idea was scary and fascinating at the same time. I imagined that I might actually have spirits that walked around with me all day like Topper did in the popular TV show at the time. Topper had two deceased friends, George and Marian Kirby, who only he could see and communicate with. The idea that I might have my own George and Marian seemed like fun. Birdie always encouraged us to get to know our guides. "Talk to them," she said, "even if you can't see them. Tell them you want a relationship with them. They will help you a lot on your journey."

But I was afraid, and getting to know my guides was a slow process. I slept with my lights on, so if they floated through the room, like my brother's guide had done, at least I wouldn't be frightened half to death — or so I hoped. I always kept a radio on because the silence scared me: I was worried that they might start talking to me. I wondered what they would sound like.

The first time I heard my guides, I was washing dishes. A very soft voice, rather like a thought, said, "My name is Theodore — but you can call me Teddy." Then a female thought came: "My name is Anna." These "voices" didn't sound very different from my thoughts. I asked them to talk to me more, but that's all they said. Birdie had told us that guides are not always chatty. They just say what's important for us to know. From that point on I kept the radio off in the house and in my car just in case they wanted to talk to me — and slowly, as my fear of them lessened, we began communicating.

My guides helped me in my psychic work and helped me understand my healing gift. Doing psychic readings seemed more acceptable back in the '70s than being a spiritual healer, so I practiced on only my family whenever they got sick and did some healings on a few trusted friends. My guides and my intuition would always help me know where to place my hands, how long to keep them there, and what to say to the person. They taught me about certain techniques and about ethics and boundaries. They helped me understand that death is a healing, a beginning and not an ending. They continually hammered in my head to keep it simple.

Over the years my guides have changed. The old ones move on to help others and new ones take their place. I've had Native American spirits who've taught me about exorcisms (clearing a person of another soul's possession), honoring Mother Earth, and some healing tools nature provides for us. In a few instances when a client is going through a difficult healing process, I've had Native American spirits come into my office and perform a healing ceremony. They sing and dance around the healing table, place herbs on different parts of the client's body, and give me step-by-step instructions where to put my hands and how long to hold them there.

Many times the spirit of Jesus has come into my office to work through my hands. One time he lifted a client's soul out of his body (while the client was sleeping) and left the room carrying it. I had a psychic vision of Jesus taking the soul to a river to cleanse it of negativity, and after he was done he returned with the man's soul and gently laid it back into his body. When my client woke up, he told me he'd had a dream that Jesus carried him to a river and cleansed him of his sins. Usually when the Native American spirits, Jesus, Yang (an ancient Chinese doctor), or various angels work with me during a session, my clients can feel their presence.

In 1983 my guides told me I needed to write a simple book that teaches others how to channel spiritual healing. I told them I knew nothing about writing books and they reassured me they would help every step of the way, which they did. My first book, *Hands That Heal*, was published in 1985 by ACS Publications and revised in 1996, updated with all the information I had learned since the first publication. In 1989 my guides told me I needed to write another book about all the unresolved emotional issues people have that cause their physical problems. That book, *Passion to Heal*, was published by Nataraj Publishing in 1993.

I also discovered in the 1970s that I have the ability to see ghosts. My brother Michael also has this ability, so we formed a brother-sister "ghostbusting" team in the 1980s and have been clearing homes of unwanted spirits for years. Because of my ghostbusting abilities, I've been on several local and national TV shows, including Sally Jesse Raphael, The Other Side, The Un-Explained, Sightings and Encounters, Strange Universe, and Looking Beyond. My family was featured on Paranormal Borderline as America's most psychic family.

As difficult as the journey has been at times, overall I feel very fortunate to have these abilities. I've had some wonderful guides who've taught me incredible things. I've had a successful psychic and healing practice for more than twenty-five years in Minneapolis. I teach beginning and advanced psychic development classes and work-shops or classes on how to channel spiritual healing.

The Evolution of This Book

This book was originally written as a ghostbusting book with bits and pieces strewn throughout about the soul and its attitude about life, death, and life after death. Publishers were interested in it, but there was always some kind of glitch and nothing would happen. Months would go by and the book would just sit on my shelf. I couldn't seem to get clear about what it needed to move forward. The only thing my guides would tell me was to be patient because timing was very important.

In the spring of 1997, I asked a psychic friend, Warren Anger, if he could get any information on what the book needed, because my agent kept calling and asking me how the manuscript was coming and I was feeling completely stuck. Warren told me that the focus of the book was all wrong and that there was a woman in my life who would help put the pieces together.

The following week I told students in my advanced psychic class that I was taking a few months off from teaching and seeing clients to finish the book I was writing on ghosts. I told them the frustrations I was going through and asked that if any of them got any psychic information on what I needed to do, to please pass it on.

When we drove home after class that evening, my teaching assistant, Sheryl Grassie, suggested to me in her wonderfully bold and knowing way that between the two of us we could get the book done the way my agent wanted it. She had grown up around writers and felt comfortable editing. Right away I thought about what Warren had said — there was a woman already in my life who would help me see what the book needed. I gave her a copy, and she called a week later to say, "I know what's wrong with this book. The focus is all wrong." I had chills all over my body. I could feel that her vision was what I was searching for.

We met for coffee, and Sheryl said she had a question for me: What was most important to me, teaching people about ghosts or about the soul? I said that the soul was most important to me, but that because all the TV shows I had been on always focused on ghosts, I thought that's what people wanted to read about. Sheryl said she felt that I needed to focus more on the soul's journey rather than on ghost stories, and she laid it out for me chapter by chapter, rearranging, changing, filling in a lot of the blanks. With Sheryl's help I was able to change the entire focus, taking out the ghost stories for later use and still retaining most of the original book.

My students always comment that they really like the stories I have, so I decided to stick with what works and share the information largely in story form. The stories in this book, then, are as close as possible to the original events, with occasional changes of minor details to protect the people involved. Most names are also changed.

For months we could not come up with a title for the book. We knew we had to be patient and wait for the title to come to us rather than come up with something that didn't fit. One day Sheryl said she was told during meditation that my name needed to be in the title of the book. She said she was also given some possible names, but had written them in her journal and would call me later. I said, "Right, my name in the title of the book? I don't think so. What would it be, *Echoes of the Soul?* Sheryl, I think you've lost it. Call me later and give me the titles that came to you." She called about two hours later and said that *Echoes of the Soul* was exactly the name she had written in her journal. The idea of putting my name in the title of the book seemed really grandiose, so for two days I tried putting it out of my mind. But it wouldn't go away. One of my spirit guides told me to look up the word echo in the dictionary. It said, "repetitive, repeats." That is exactly what the soul does. It repeats life over and over, experience after experience, until it achieves perfection.

This book is about the soul and its entire journey, from conception to completion. It answers a lot of questions many of us have had: When does the soul enter the body? What does the soul think about the birth experience? What is the soul's attitude about life on earth?

What does the soul really feel about death of the physical body and where does it go? Does the soul fear death? What does the soul do after its body has died? Does the soul meet with loved ones after death? Is there really a hell? What about reincarnation? Does it exist? What does the soul think about it? And last but not least, who and what is God and where does He fit in?*

We are all so much more than just our physical bodies — and my hope is that you'll have a deeper love, respect, and understanding of yourself, of other people, and of God when you're finished reading this book.

---

* Most of us have been raised with a male concept of God, and I find it much easier to refer to God as male throughout this book — even though I've come to know that God is a perfect balance of male and female energy.

Chapter 1

The Soul

The human body is the best picture of the human soul.

— Ludwig Wittgenstein

Before we take an in-depth look at the soul's perspective of birth, life on earth, physical death, and life after death, it's important to define just what a soul really is and answer some common questions: Does everyone have one? What does it look like? Does it die?

Webster's defines the soul as "an entity without material reality, regarded as the spiritual part of a person." I agree with Webster except that I would take it a step further and say that the soul is the spiritual part of us, which never dies.

Meeting a Soul

The first time I saw a soul *that I realized was a soul* was when I was doing a healing on a fourteen-year-old boy who had fallen eighteen feet and had landed on his head. He was hospitalized and in a coma, and the doctors gave him a bleak prognosis. I was standing over his body with my hands on his chest channeling healing energy into him. Out of nowhere I heard a male voice from behind me say, "Please heal the speech part of my brain. I'd like to talk again." I felt a bit unnerved because I knew there was no one else in the room with me. I slowly turned and saw, in the corner of the room, a transparent carbon copy of the young man I had my hands on.

I asked him who he was, and he told me he was the soul that lived inside the boy's body. I was so surprised by what I was hearing and seeing! I asked why he was out of his body, and he told me it wasn't unusual for a soul to go out of its body and take an occasional break. He also said that when the soul is out, the body doesn't feel any pain. He again asked me to work on the speech part of the brain and then floated out of the room.

The boy was completely still, his breathing very shallow. While I channeled the healing, my mind was trying to find a rational explanation of what just happened. I wondered for a quick second if I hadn't somehow imagined it. Then just as quickly as the soul had left the room, he reentered and moved back into his body. I could now feel a life force in the body that had been absent just a moment before. The boy started moving. His breathing became normal, and he began moaning in pain. I told him that I didn't know which part of the brain controlled speech, and his arm raised off the bed and came down on the front part of his head. (The nurse later confirmed that this was indeed the area of the brain that controlled speech!)

This boy's soul continued to come in and go out of his body

throughout the healing process and continued to communicate to me whenever he felt the need.

Since that night, I've met hundreds of souls who have worked with me in various ways and have taught me everything that I am passing on to you.

Creating Souls

Every human being has a soul. We think in terms of the soul being somehow separate from us when, in fact, it's not at all. Our souls are made of energy. They are beings of light. They can take on any shape they want. Most of the souls I have communicated with appear in human form, but I have also seen them appear as streaks of light or blobs of energy. In whatever form the soul appears, it is a thinking, feeling being with memories, unresolved issues, and a sense of humor. It is totally alive energy.

When God created us, He created our souls and then breathed life into each of us by putting a part of Himself (or Divine Spirit) within us. This is where the term Higher Self comes from. It is the part of our souls infused with the Holy Spirit. Within that part or light is a voice that guides us throughout our lives, often referred to as the "still, small voice within."

When our souls are created, we live on the other side with God and receive the nurturing that we need in order to give us a good foundation. There comes a certain point in our development (similar to a baby's development) when we want to begin learning and growing, and this is when the cycle of lifetimes begins.

Because there is already perfection on the other side, God created this world for us to come to, like a school away from home, to do our learning here. The objective is to develop ourselves and our world to our highest potential. We were given an unlimited amount of time to do this, and have been given as many different lifetimes as we need in order to learn all that's possible to fulfill our potential to the fullest.

If we understood what this really means, so many of us would live our lives differently. God has created us from *Himself*, from His image and likeness. We have unlimited potential! Our souls were created *carte blanche*, which means we have full authority to become the very best we can be.

Whenever I give a talk on this subject, people think I'm talking about their bodies. They say things like, "Not me, I've got short legs, I could never be a basketball player." "Not me, I flunked out of high school and can't even get a decent job." "God didn't create me with unlimited potential 'cause I'm physically challenged . . . I'm too stupid . . . I'm too poor. . . . "

I am not talking about the body, although that, too, has incredible potential. I'm talking about the soul each of us has — the real "us" inside. We all have bodies, which house souls, which contain Divine Spirit, or God. It is the Divine Spirit within our souls that gives life. Without the Divine Spark, our souls are simply energy, just as our bodies are empty shells without our souls.

There are differing beliefs about whether God created our souls all at the same time (ten billion or so years ago) or if He continues to create new souls along the way. My inner knowingness says God has continued to create new souls — which explains why our population continues to grow. You'll hear references to old souls and new souls — an old soul has had many lifetimes and has gained quite a bit of wisdom in doing so, whereas a new soul hasn't had many lives and is still in the process of gaining wisdom. I can tell by looking into the eyes of a newborn baby if its soul is old or relatively new. The older soul has that knowingness as if to say, "I'm back," and the newer soul has a less aware look. Either way, that baby's body has a soul in it and that soul has a purpose for being on earth.

Soul Travel

When a soul resides in a body, it is attached to that body by a silver cord, similar to the umbilical cord. The cord keeps the soul connected to the body throughout its lifetime and is severed only at the time of physical death. It in no way restricts the soul, which has the freedom to come and go whenever it chooses to. The cord also has no limit as to how far it can stretch, so the soul is not bound by anything except the conscious mind.

I know that soul travel or astral projection bothers some people. We don't like thinking that we can't control the soul, but whether we like it or not, it is something our soul does all the time. Most soul travel takes place at night when the body is sleeping, but the soul also takes little quick trips in and out of the body during the day. As you will continually learn throughout this book, most of us are not conscious of what goes on with our souls, and that's usually how both the body and the soul prefer it.

Signs of an Out-of-Body Experience

Here are some signs that indicate your soul is having an out-of-body experience. They are not, however, exclusive to soul travel.

- You're sleeping at night and your body jerks hard. You wake up for a quick second, but go right back to sleep.

- You have flying dreams that feel very real.

- You wake up in the middle of the night and you can't open your eyes or move your body. You want to talk or yell to someone that your body seems frozen, but you can't get your mouth to move.

- You have brief periods throughout the day when you seem to go blank (daydreaming).

- You have very real dreams of visiting a deceased loved one.

- You dream of being with a loved one who lives far away and you wake feeling sad because it felt like you had to leave that person.

Most out-of-body experiences are at night so as not to upset us consciously. As you will see in each chapter, the soul prefers to remain somewhat anonymous because it usually has its own agenda. Many times when I've communicated with a client's soul, it has asked me not to tell the body what it's up to because the body (the conscious mind) wouldn't understand. The reason for this is simply because the soul looks at every experience it goes through as a tool for learning and is usually emotionally detached from it, whereas those of us in a body usually react in some way emotionally to the experiences we go through.

When the Soul Travels

Maybe you're wondering why and where the soul travels and what it does when it's out of the body. How many times do we find ourselves saying that we wish we could be in two places at once? The truth is that we can be in two places at the same time, but we're just not conscious of it. Some examples:

- If you have a sick loved one you can't get to, your soul will visit the person, whether he or she is in a different part of town or the world.

- If you're a parent who had to send a possible sick child to school, your soul may check on the child throughout the day.

- If there's someone you love, you may leave your body to give the person a kiss or a hug. (No, the person wouldn't consciously feel it, but he or she would get a feeling of being loved.)

- Your soul may give a pep talk to a loved one about to give a presentation at work or to a student about to take a test.

- When two people need you at the same time, your soul may visit one of them.

- If you have to be at work but would rather be home or shopping or fishing, your soul can take quick little trips to your favorite fishing hole or shopping mall just to take a little break in the middle of a hectic day.

- If you take your car in for repairs and want to know what is *really* being done to it, your soul may visit your auto mechanic.

- A healer's soul may go out and channel a healing to someone.

- If there's a function such as a concert or play you can't attend, your soul may go anyway.

- If you are bored in a classroom, your soul may go somewhere it would rather be.

- If a person is in a relationship with someone who lives in a different place geographically, one soul may travel to the other soul to spend the night. The souls may take turns each night.

- If a parent has children in other parts of the world, the parent's soul may travel at night to see how the children are.

- If there's a part of the world that you love, but because of your lifestyle you can't possibly move there, your soul may visit that location frequently.

- When your body becomes really stressed from all the hustle and bustle of life but you can't manage a vacation, your soul may go to a favorite spot such as the mountains, ocean, or countryside to spend the night. In the morning, your body feels better and isn't conscious of the reasons why. Sometimes the experience comes through as a dream and you wake up feeling refreshed because you "dreamt" about your favorite vacation spot.

• When you are in your dying process, your soul goes in and out quite a bit. It may be going to those still living to communicate with their souls. If there are amends to be made, conversations to be had, instructions to work out, anything your soul feels is important to take care of before leaving, these things will take place. Your soul may also be going from this side to the other side to prepare a home for itself.

• If you go to bed struggling with an answer to a problem, no matter how simple or complex, your soul may go out and talk to other souls about possible solutions. When you wake up in the morning, you may discover you have the answer.

• Your soul may leave your body at night to spend time with your spirit guides (discussed in more detail in chapter 4). You may be surprised to know we communicate with our spirit guides daily.

• The soul might feel the need to leave if there is any kind of abuse — physical, mental, emotional, or sexual — taking place. When the abuse is about to start, the soul will leave the room and return after the abuse has ended. The professionals call this *disassociation*. Years later this person may go to therapy about abuse issues, but will be unable to remember specific incidents. This can make recovery more difficult, but not impossible.

Sheryl (my editor) and I were sitting in a restaurant one day working on the book. Suddenly she got that blank stare that can indicate the soul has left. Within fifteen seconds she "came to" and apologized for being so spacey. I asked if she was concerned about one of her children, and she said that her daughter wasn't happy at her day-care center. I said that her soul was probably checking to see how her daughter was feeling because parents' souls will do that throughout the day when they worry there may be a problem. When Sheryl got home there was a call from the day-care center indicating there had been a problem that morning.

If we are concerned about a person or a situation we can't physically get to, our souls will check it out. The problem that can arise for our souls is how to get our conscious attention to the matter. We may feel an internal agitation about something or feel compelled to call someone, but unfortunately a lot of us don't act on these feelings because there's no rational reason to back up what we're feeling. By making people more aware of this, I'm hoping they'll start to pay more attention to what they *know* inside.

Signs That Other Souls Are Traveling

We've looked at signs that indicate when you're out of your body, but how can we tell if others are out of body, and what can we do about it?

- If they are sleeping, their bodies will be extremely still. There's no movement at all and the breathing is very shallow.

- If they are awake, they will go blank for a few seconds. The eyes are open but it appears as if no one's there. "The lights are on, but nobody's home."

If you encounter either of these experiences, don't panic. Just let the person be. Our souls are very wise and wouldn't go out unless they felt the need. I strongly suggest you do not shake the person or make the person wake up. It can be hard for the body if someone is pulling on it while the soul is out. The body usually wakes up disoriented and cranky.

Out-of-body experiences are fascinating to read about. Robert Monroe's books are my favorite on the subject, but I know there are other good books as well. (See Recommended Reading.)

Soul Loss

Soul loss can occur if a soul has had to disassociate itself from its body a lot. When a person has suffered a lot of abuse or loss, a part of the soul may leave in order to cope. That soul part may or may not return after the abuse has ended. If the abuse continues for years, if there is a problem with chemical abuse, or if there is something else traumatic the person couldn't cope with, several parts of the soul may disassociate. That person then becomes quite *fragmented.*

I'd like to share an experience to help relay this concept a little better. As far back as I can remember, I had always felt that something was missing in my life, but I had no idea what it was or how to put words to it. I had suffered with depression most of my life and no matter how many therapists I went to to overcome it, the depression had always come back.

A psychic friend of mine suggested I see a shaman for possible soul loss, which at the time sounded a little weird to me. But I was so tired of fighting the depression, that I was ready to try anything.

We have some wonderful shamans in Minneapolis, and among them is a gifted man named Timothy Cope. Timothy is one of those rare people who is quite humble about his gifts. I have the highest regard for him and his work.

The day I went for my "soul retrieval," as the shamans call it, I had no idea what to expect. Timothy asked me not to tell him anything about why I had come. He said he would go on his shamanic journey first to see if any parts of my soul had left. If they had, he would ask those parts what they needed to reconnect, and then he would bring them back. He said that then I could tell him why I had come, but he didn't want to be influenced by anything I said.

The next forty-five minutes are hard to describe. It was a very mystical experience. Timothy played drumming music and prayed. He burned sage. He called in spirits to help him on his journey and then lay next to me on the floor. He was silent for several minutes and then explained that he retrieved a part of my soul that had been missing since I was four (I was forty-four when this experience happened). He told me an important man in my life had died when I was four years old and I couldn't stand being without him, so a part of my soul had gone to live with him on the other side. He said he had found me holding this man's hand and that he suspected it was my grandfather.

I was shocked by what Timothy said, because it was true. My grandpa, whom I had adored and who had taken care of me every day when I was little, died when I was four years old. Timothy suggested I find a nurturing male that would give to my inner child the love my grandpa had given to me all those years ago. Timothy said a prayer that I would find such a person and have those needs met. Within a couple of weeks, I met Jeffrey Maxwell at a conference at the Ozark Research Institute who became that person in my life. Even though we were together only for two days, we've continued to correspond for years. Jeff continues to be one of the people in my life who nurtures my inner child.

Another positive outcome from the soul retrieval was the decrease and eventual end to my depression. I no longer felt that a part of me was missing. I felt whole for the first time.

I'd like to reassure you that if there are parts of your soul that have become fragmented, the soul has a great intelligence and wisdom and can find the resources to help itself heal. If, after reading this section, you feel led to seek a shaman for possible soul retrieval, I recommend you act on that feeling or intuitive voice.

I suggest reading *Soul Retrieval,* by Sandra Ingerman. Also call your local New Age bookstore and ask if there are any reputable shamans in your area. There are many good sources that can help you find the right books and the right shaman if this is something you suspect you may need.

To Summarize:

- Everyone has a soul, which is made of energy. This energy comes from God.

- The soul looks very similar to the current body it's living in. For those souls who have left their physical bodies (died), they look like the last body they resided in.

- There is a voice within every soul that guides that soul through its lifetimes. This voice is commonly referred to as intuition.

- Souls are attached to the physical bodies they reside in by silver cords, which are severed only at the time of death.

- The soul has the ability to come and go from the body at will — this is called astral projection or out-of-body experiences.

- Soul loss can occur: The soul can become fragmented from trauma and needs to be restored to feel complete.

Chapter 2

Heaven: The Other Side

There is no death. Only a change of worlds.

— Chief Seattle

It was the beginning of spring in 1992. The sun was shining, birds were singing, earth was coming alive again after a long winter in Minnesota. It was Palm Sunday and I was torn between going to church and doing what I wanted to do, which was preparing my garden for planting. I felt like I should be in church, but I needed to be in the quiet of my yard and talk to God there. I decided to pass on church and spend that very special time outside.

My brother Michael and I had been on a ghostbusting job the previous night, and I went to bed thinking about the other side of the veil. When I woke up that Sunday morning, it was still on my mind. As I was working in my garden, I was thinking of the knowledge about heaven I had gained over the years. I had learned quite a bit from readings I had channeled and had gathered bits and pieces while communicating with the deceased, but I had no real, experiential knowledge. I had been ghostbusting for twenty years and had believed I was sending those souls to a good place, but for some reason that day, I wanted more concrete information.

As I worked in the garden, I asked God if I could please have more knowledge about the other side. I told Him that with all the work I did about death and life after death, I would like to give more information to people about heaven and where they go when they die. I told God that I wouldn't ask Him about it more than this one time, but I was very open to receiving any knowledge. I was curious as to how He might give me this information, but decided to let it go and see what might happen.

Three days later, after completely forgetting the prayer, I had the most memorable experience of my career. It was Wednesday; I had just finished a healing session with Neil, a good friend, and he was heading upstairs from my basement office. My office started to fill with a hazy white energy. I felt strange — weak, as if I was going to collapse. My body seemed like it had fallen asleep, yet I was awake. I was beginning to have an out-of-body experience, but I didn't recognize it right away.

I became aware of a woman, in spirit form, standing in front of me. I couldn't see her face, just the back of her head and her long blonde hair. She said to me, "Let's go, let's go." I felt afraid and asked Neil if he would help me. I told him something very strange was happening and that a presence was urging me to follow her.

My perception was completely off. I knew on one level I was in my office, but I also felt as if I were in another dimension. Neil shook my body, hoping to stop whatever it was that was happening. It did stop for about fifteen seconds, and then it started again — the blonde spirit appeared in front of me and prompted me to go with her. The feeling I had was familiar — I told Neil it felt as if I were dying. The room continued to fill with white fog, and my body became so weak that I wanted to just lie down and let go.

Then I became aware of a tunnel directly in front of me. It was the same tunnel I had seen in so many of my ghostbusting jobs — the one I send the ghosts through and into the light, the tunnel that connects our side to the other side.

One of my spirit guides told me to have Neil call my brother Michael and ask him to come over as quickly as possible, then to get me upstairs and into the living room. Neil called Michael and then dragged me upstairs. By this point I could barely speak, and my legs appeared lifeless. Neil kept telling me to get back into my body and the blonde spirit kept telling me to go with her. He dragged me to the couch, and my body fell into a heap. I felt as if I had no control over what was happening.

Minutes seemed like hours as we waited for my brother to arrive. When Michael finally came, he was fully aware of what was happening. He had talked with his guides on the drive over, and they told him that three days earlier I had asked God to go to the other side. They told him I was being allowed to go and would consciously remember the experience.

He said, "Echo, I am supposed to hold your hand and ground your body while your soul goes to the other side and gathers information."

As he was talking I finally realized that I was having an out-of-body experience and that the blonde spirit was my soul trying to get me to let go and move to the other side. I had not told anyone, including my brother, about my prayer on Sunday, so I was amazed at what he said and what was happening.

The Other Side

Michael took my hand and told me that everything was fine, that I should go, and that he would be here to protect my body. With his reassurance, I fully left my body, and my conscious mind merged with the blonde spirit that was my soul. I started to float though the tunnel. A loving warmth surrounded me as I moved more fully into it. All throughout the tunnel I could hear a faint voice echoing, "Let go, let go."

Many souls were in the tunnel waiting to greet departing (dying) loved ones. Reunions were taking place around me. Then I saw a bright light ahead, at the end of the tunnel. I floated up, going higher and higher. As I came up to the white light, I remember thinking that I should close my eyes or I would be blinded from its brightness — but I opened my eyes instead and flowed right through it.

I came out on the other side feeling calm and aware. I could see a quaint little village with cobblestone streets. My grandmother was standing there with a friend. She introduced me, and her friend said, "Oh, you didn't tell me she was dying today," and my grandmother said, "Oh no, she's not dying, just visiting." I looked closely at my grandma's face. She looked so beautiful — no wrinkles, no stress, just joy. A youthfulness and serenity engulfed her. I looked around and saw several old friends who had died. They didn't come over to me. They just smiled as if they knew I was not to waste any time. They all had that same youthful, serene look on their faces.

Out of nowhere an angel appeared. She was quite lovely with light, wavy, reddish hair down to her shoulders, a long flowing gown, and, yes, wings. She told me she would be my guide and wanted to show me as much as possible in the limited time we had.

The first place she took me to was called the Pink Place. The entire community had a pink aura around it. It was beautiful. In front of us was a hospital, and even though we were standing some distance from it, I could see inside. It wasn't like a hospital on earth with a lot of medical equipment and personnel. It was more like a resting place, with caregivers. They were not necessarily doctors or nurses, just simply helpers.

Some souls in the hospital were going through an adjustment period, learning to live without their physical bodies. Many had been heavily medicated during their death process and their souls were affected by the drugs. They were resting, healing, and adjusting. Some souls had difficulty accepting their deaths, and caregivers were working with them to help them accept their transition. Some souls from physically handicapped bodies needed help adjusting to life without challenged bodies. A large section of the hospital was for suicide victims. Some were asleep, others were dealing with the frustration of taking their lives. Many were still knocked out from the amount of drugs or alcohol they took to cause their deaths.

There were many floors to the hospital, but I didn't have time to investigate. I needed to move on. I saw many souls lying on the grass outside the hospital with their eyes closed. The angel said the Pink Place was for healing and that those souls were healing from the energy that surrounded the community.

Then, we floated down a road. First I saw a landscape with rolling hills, lush foliage, grass, flowers, streams, lakes, and rivers. The colors of the flowers were crisp and vivid, and the flowers all smelled fragrant. We continued floating over a hill and into a valley, where I saw a huge white and gold coliseum with enormous pillars, windows, and doors, but no glass. I saw angels coming in and out. The angel told me that this is where the angels live who help people on earth.

About this time I could faintly hear my brother's voice. He was telling me, "Go find the music." Then I was aware that there was music playing all around me. I looked at the angel and she motioned me to follow her. We floated to a meadow of singers and musicians. I saw — of all people! — Nat King Cole, and then many others that I recognized from this side. Some were writing songs, some were singing. This is a little hard to describe, but there were several kinds of music being played at the same time. It was like a giant radio station, and all you had to do was "tune into the vibration" you wanted to hear.

The next city we floated to was particularly important to me. Ever since I was a little girl, Jesus has always been a central figure in my life. Perhaps that's why the angel took me where she did. Or perhaps it was because Easter week was being celebrated on earth. In any case, we were now in a magnificent place, truly a place of beauty. It was very picturesque — blue sky, lush green nature everywhere. Thousands of souls were milling around, very excited about something. It felt as if a celebration were going on; people were very emotional, some cheering, others crying. Still others stood off by themselves, completely captivated by the man in the middle of the crowd. He was speaking or teaching about something. I looked at the angel as if to ask her who the man was, and she said it was Jesus. I wondered if it was okay for me to be there. The angel, reading my thoughts, told me it was fine. I was welcome. She had wanted me to experience the City of Jesus (as she called it), knowing what He meant to me.

I felt great joy and awe as I watched Him preach. Here was the man I cherished so much. He was surrounded by a golden aura that radiated wisdom and knowledge. His features were striking — dark shoulder-length hair, a beard, a tanned complexion, and the most intense eyes I had ever seen. Yet the thing I found myself mesmerized by were His hands: strong, weathered, thousands of years old, full of wisdom and knowledge about all the pain He had healed.

He talked to an enormous crowd of souls about loving one another. His whole message, His whole essence, was love. There was such a gentleness about Him. He felt so powerful, and yet He was humble. I wanted to get as close to Him as possible. I remember feeling as if I were truly Home, and I didn't want to leave this magnificent city. Everywhere I looked the air seemed charged with hope, with answers.

I could hear my name being called — "Echo, Echo" — over and over. My brother was urging me to return to my body because this experience was very hard on it, but I didn't want to leave. Then Michael told me to look for God, and it was then I realized that I was surrounded by God. God was and is everywhere. Just think the word God and He's there. A presence. A knowingness. It is very difficult to describe.

Again Michael urged me to come back. I asked the angel what else she could teach me before I returned to my body.

She told me that heaven was full of communities and that each reflected a different reality. The reality we live by on earth, the consciousness we hold, determines where we go in heaven. For example, if during your lifetime you were a hard-working, devout Catholic, when you go to heaven you will live in a community that embraces the same beliefs. She showed me a community of beggars and thieves. She said that is their reality. All day long they steal or beg from one another. Eventually they will grow tired of that way of life and start asking others outside their community if there is a better way to live. All souls continually move on to different realities, always searching for a better way. People need to evolve in their beliefs in heaven just as they must on earth. Each soul needs to learn and grow toward its oneness with God.

The angel told me that in heaven each community has a classroom and an instructor who teaches the reality of that group. As souls advance, there is no longer a need for some communities and they will no longer exist.

I said that it seemed so complicated to have so many communities with varying realities. She said that it is actually less complicated than it is on earth, for in heaven everyone is clear about each other's reality. If you live in a community different from others, you have a different belief system than they do. It's that simple. She said that it's more complex on earth because we believe that we all have the same reality when, in fact, we don't. She said that's why we have so many problems on earth, because we have trouble honoring each other's convictions. We don't want to accept that everyone has a different reality; we want everyone to be and think and act like us.

I asked the angel about movie stars because I am such a movie buff. She said that they also have their community and may live there if they choose to remain that star. Some who cross over desire a change from their movie star identity and go to a community that better reflects their individuality and reality. (I saw John F. Kennedy's soul while I was doing a reading for someone. I asked him how long he was going to remain JFK, and he told me that as long as there was a need for people to meet him, he would remain on the other side rather than reincarnate. He told me that he was one of the first people, after relatives, people ask to meet. He showed me an image of himself shaking many hands, greeting people, and enjoying what he was doing. Many people ask me if I have seen Elvis, and, yes, I have. He's on the other side, and he's looking good!)

The comedian Sam Kinnison had died about two weeks before this experience happened. I am a Kinnison fan and was curious to know how he was doing. I asked the angel about him and she motioned me to an area where I saw him standing on a road. I could hear his laughter, and I felt happy to hear him laughing again. There were many souls around him, shaking his hand, congratulating him on doing such a good job while he was on earth. I looked at the angel, somewhat baffled by what they were saying, because in my mind Sam was kind of crude in his performances and it surprised me that they were saying he did such a good job. The angel smiled and told me that he did indeed accomplish what he came to earth to do. She said that his job was to get people to think about their beliefs, their values, their morals. She said that yes, he was somewhat crude in his delivery, but it accomplished what it was supposed to. People would walk away from his performances thinking about the things he had said and questioning their beliefs.

As I watched him in his big overcoat, beret, and tennis shoes, shaking hands and laughing with people, I heard my brother again, sternly calling me back. My body was having a difficult time. I could tell by the tone of his voice that I had to go, and I quickly flowed back to the light. To my right I saw a broad stairway, and I asked the angel where it led. She said that there are several levels to heaven. The highest level is where we all have the same reality, where we know we are one with God and we live in peace with one another. During several readings I have done since that day, I have briefly seen that level. There are many souls there, all knowing their oneness with one another and with God. It is magnificent. I have been able to see it only for a short time, but just as with the City of Jesus, I did not want to let it go.

I asked the angel one last question. Was the village with the cobblestone streets, where I had arrived, the entrance point into heaven? She said it was one of many places throughout heaven where people arrived. Some went directly to the hospital, others went to entry points determined by their consciousnesses. She said that she wished she could teach me and show me so much more, but my body was really suffering and I had to go back. As soon as she spoke those words, my soul jolted back into my body.

When I took this conscious journey out of my body, I used all the energy in my soul to do it. My body experienced a great deal of difficulty while I was out. I was like a rag doll, lifeless and limp. After my soul came back in, it took at least twenty minutes before I could speak. My tongue was thick, my eyes were hard to open and very sensitive to light. It was a great effort to move my body for some time. At least an hour passed before I felt normal again. As soon as I was able to go to bed, I slept for twelve hours.

The Higher Level

The days that followed were somewhat difficult. I didn't want to be here anymore. I wished I could be on the other side; it felt like Home and I missed it. I could understand the ambivalence I have seen in souls who are preparing to reincarnate. They would stay also, but know the opportunities to advance quickly are on earth so this is the place they come to.

Five years have passed since my conscious journey to heaven, and my ability to see the other side has continued to grow stronger. I've wanted to climb the ladder and go to the higher levels, but I have been told many times that I would be allowed to go only when I was able to understand what I saw.

In May 1997 my very dear friend and spiritual advisor, Rev. Phil Laporte, died from cancer. I was very aware of his presence at the funeral, but didn't see him again until about three months later. When I saw him, I understood what the guides meant when they said I must to be able to accept what I saw before I could see it. When Phil appeared to me he was an essence, not a form. The best way to describe it is that it looked almost like clear Jello. I could see it. It moved. In one sense it appeared solid, but then again, it seemed flimsy, almost not real.

The way he first appeared was in thought. I got a very strong mental image of him; it made me stop what I was doing and put myself on pause. Then I saw a bloblike energy. It is so difficult to describe. I said, out loud, "Phil, is that you?" Then I clearly heard his voice say, "Yes, it's me." I asked him why he wasn't in a form like everyone else I had seen on the other side, and he said that his vibration or energy was very light and that he was an essence. He told me he could make himself become a form if it was necessary for me to believe it was him, but I *knew* it was him and told him it wasn't necessary.

He told me he was going to live on another level in heaven. He said that I had visited level four and he would be living on level five, although he hadn't fully transitioned to it yet. He said that he went back and forth between the two levels because his family members and many of his loved ones lived on level four.

I told him I wanted to put as much information as I could about heaven in the book and asked him if he could teach me about level five. He told me I needed to prepare myself physically and mentally, and when I was ready I would be shown level five.

Some months later I could finally open psychically and see level five without doing another conscious soul journey. I projected my mind there, much like remote viewing. I saw level four and then saw an open door that led to the next level. An angel led me on this journey. Like Phil, she was an essence.

The angel pointed to the open door and said to follow her. She said the door is open all the time to anyone who wants to go to the next level, but only those that have grown spiritually can see the door. There were many angels around, and they were of a different vibrational level than the angels on level four. They appeared more serious. There was also a more intense feeling on that level, yet the energy felt much lighter. The word *fluid* comes to mind. Everything seemed to flow. The angel told to me that level-five beings can change from essence to form anytime they want, but they don't see a need. They moved like fluid. Their vibration was higher, more intense, and yet the whole feeling was so much lighter. When I compared it to level four, level four seemed much heavier, and when I compared it to earth, earth was amazingly heavier. No wonder it's hard for some souls when they first come to earth.

I asked the angel how she would describe the lighter energy, and she said it was much more God-like or spiritual on level five, that each level's energy is more and more God-like until we reach the level seven, which is completely the pure energy of God. She said level five is the beginning of Nirvana, and that when a soul has fully moved into that level it doesn't reincarnate. Although the soul has an option of reincarnation, it chooses not to because the vibration is so heavy on earth. There is an overall feeling on level five of growth, of teaching and learning, and many souls there are teachers or guides for us.

She said level four souls still have karma, or life lessons to experience. They will still reincarnate. Level five souls have all their karma cleaned and have healed all their personal pain. She says there are some souls that could move to level five but choose to come back to earth one more time to be examples of how to live our lives. These are the people we consider angels on earth. They are finished with karma and are simply here to help us grow.

There are no resentments on level five. No blaming of God or others. No immaturity such as competition or rebelliousness. No feelings of lack or limitation. The souls understand abundance and how it's created. They truly know themselves and one another, and their focus is to continually bring harmony to all. They fully comprehend their responsibility to the whole of humankind and do their part to help everyone to become one. These souls have a deep understanding of their oneness with God and flow with it. There's an acknowledgment of the partnership they have with their source and they respect it and act accordingly.

The angel went on to say that communication is through telepathy. There is no need to open our mouths on level five, or to breathe. She said something about fluids and water that I didn't fully understand — something about being more a part of the water, but a different kind of water than we know on earth. She said we don't fully understand the concept of water yet. We think we do, but our understanding is primitive.

There is no grieving on level five — it ends on level four. There is a level of forgiveness on level five that is foreign to us. There are different laws on the higher levels that we honor because we desire order, in every way, not chaos.

The environment on the level five is similar to level four except that it is even more beautiful. Lush nature is everywhere. The colors seemed more subtle, softer. There is a strong, pervasive feeling of love throughout. I wondered if it's because these souls no longer have karma so they can choose to focus on things that are important to them. Whatever the reason, there is a noticeable calmness, a serenity, on level five that isn't on level four.

The angel told me that my friend Phil has chosen to teach level four souls how to get to level five without coming back to earth. He sees how draining earth is to the soul, and he never wants to come back to this heavy energy. He wants to spare others the same thing. The angel said that this is typical of a level five souls: They are interested in healing humanity.

I asked if she can teach me about level six, and she said it would not be easy for me to grasp. The one glimmer I got is that level six takes us deeper into the heart of God, into knowing God more fully before we go to the highest level where we become one with the Creator again.

I became more curious about all levels of heaven and asked the angel if she could explain each level in more detail. Instead of describing each level, she explained the different levels of souls and said they reflected what each level in heaven was like.

Levels of Souls

Level one souls are totally self-absorbed. They are completely unaware that there is a connection among all living things. They are totally focused on their survival. They live in fear. They believe there isn't enough to go around, so they take whatever they want.

The angel said we are all created with an inner knowing that tells us the difference between right and wrong, but level one souls choose to bypass this instinct. They live as if this life were the only one they'll ever have and believe that the Law of Karma — Do unto others as you would have them do unto you — does not apply to them. They see themselves as completely separate from others and believe both secular laws and spiritual laws do not apply to them. Level one souls have no belief in a power outside themselves. They have not begun to love in the greater sense of the word. They treat people, animals, and nature in a primitive manner, taking whatever they want for their own gratification and having no concern for others. Level one is when the soul's karma begins.

Level two souls begin to open their hearts to others. They are less self-absorbed, less fearful, yet most of the time they exist in a place similar to level one. Level two souls open slowly to the possibility that they are not completely alone. They stop looking at others as unimportant or as threats to their survival. These souls cautiously begin to reach out to people, animals, or nature around them. They learn a great deal on level two, yet they forget, too, over and over, and revert to their old ways.

Level three souls continue to grow, understanding and remembering more of their oneness with humanity and their connection to God. At level three the connection to God is through their religion. These souls gravitate to the philosophy of a God of shame and punishment. They begin to understand the Law of Karma, to know that they can't hurt others without being held accountable. They vacillate among fear of survival, fear of others, and fear of God, and, in the process they begin to learn to trust. They take their first tentative steps in a positive direction, moving away from their self-absorbed fearful states into broader, yet more inclusive belief systems. These souls take risks with more than just one person or animal and move into a new arena in which they discover the similarities between themselves and others, rather than focus on why they are separate from others.

Souls on level four strive to understand their oneness with all living beings, animal and human, and with God, and they try to live their lives accordingly. They have had many difficult lifetimes on levels one, two, and three, and are now searching for help, desiring a greater understanding about all of life. They ask more questions, read more books, and begin their spiritual quest.

Souls on all four levels suffer from many addictions in the physical world, but recovery from those addictions usually occurs on level four. Addictions, on the soul's level, can be seen as an ongoing part of the battle between the physical realm and the spiritual realm to determine which is ultimately in power.

Level four souls usually make great strides in their lives, transitioning from their old beliefs to new, more solid ones. They begin to realize that the physical world is temporary, and they learn to detach from its importance. They also have more enjoyment from what they own because they know possessions are temporary. These souls see the wisdom in their life lessons, and they welcome them and grow because of them. They see tremendous progress in themselves, and they open their arms to other people, animals, nature, and God. They step away from religion and move into spirituality. They crave less physically and more spiritually, yearning for the truth about life, death, and God.

By the time level four souls are ready to move to level five, all problems from levels one, two, three, and four have healed. Karma is completed. All negative acts have been amended, and the soul has a much greater understanding of its spiritual journey. On level five souls no longer want for anything. They are open to change, to new concepts, and they take responsibility for their lives. They have a consciousness, a greater awareness, about life on earth. They feel a responsibility to clean things up, to teach others. They have a desire to continually evolve. The more they grow, the more they want to understand.

Level five souls understand their oneness with all of creation and with God. One reason these souls do not return to earth is that struggle and conflict of any kind is no longer in their consciousnesses. They are like angels: they have completely moved out of fear, war, hatred, and poverty. They have shifted tremendously and are focused on healing through love, abundance, and God.

Level six souls live in a blissful state, nothing like life on earth. We can only imagine what true bliss is because we equate everything with the physical body or with earthly life. Level six is far beyond earth. Level six souls experience a complete letting go of physical conscious-ness and a complete opening up to level seven, the highest level.

Then the angel smiled and said that level seven is retirement in the truest sense. With that she ended the description. She also said that we live many, many lifetimes on each level. For example, we may have twenty lives in a level one consciousness, which is why we create so much bad karma for ourselves. We may have thirty lifetimes on level two before we understand that there is another way to live and believe. We move onto the next level and may have twenty lives, more or less, on level three, then another twenty or so on level four.

Because level four is our last level on earth, we may have the most lifetimes on that level before we fully grow into a higher consciousness and clean up all our karma from previous lifetimes. The angel said that level four lives are usually pretty intense because we have more knowledge and are more awakened to what we're doing. She said that souls move in and out of lower levels until they remain solid in their level four beliefs. Then they begin the process of letting go to move on to higher levels.

This is probably what the angel meant when she said we grieve on level four but not on level five. Level five souls have moved through their attachment to earth and to their lives on earth. They are looking only upward to "retirement." I easily liken levels one, two, and three to day care, nursery school, and kindergarten. After we move to the higher levels, we seldom look back because our focus is on growing up in consciousness.

In the first chapter, I mentioned old souls and new souls. A new soul is at level one. An old soul is at level four. You may wonder which level you're on. My guess is that no one on levels one and two would be drawn to this book. Level three souls may read it, but will probably feel confusion because of their religious beliefs versus the contents of this book. Level four souls will be drawn to it because they're searching and want to understand themselves and their lives better.

The part of heaven I visited has souls on levels one through four living there, just as we do here on earth. We all exist together and yet, just as in heaven, we each live in our own communities. We can look at people in our lives and see that, generally, they fit in one of the four levels. The angel said that she had hesitated before giving me the information because we on earth have a tendency to be judgmental of ourselves and others, and this tendency could distract us from focusing on ourselves. Remember that all of us on levels one through four help one another to keep moving upward. We show one another where we've been, where we are now, and what the possibilities of advancement are — what our potential is. We can see in one another what our worst qualities are and what our best capabilities can be.

The beggars and thieves eventually understand that they can obtain food and possessions in ways other than stealing or begging, and they start pursuing alternatives, eventually moving on. They begin to grow in consciousness. That's how all of us grow and heal. We use both the negative and positive examples shown by others. Everyone around us reflects some part of us to ourselves. That's why we're all here together, to help one another heal and grow.

Chapter 3

Birth: Going Back to School

We are not human beings having a spiritual experience.
We are spiritual beings having a human experience.

— Pierre Teilhard de Chardin

Birth is such a wonderful event. New life. New beginnings. I love watching people open their hearts when a baby comes into the world. Unfortunately, most of us have forgotten what's really going on when a baby is born. We treat babies like empty vessels lacking in knowledge, dreams, or aspirations — but the truth is, the soul that is born to each body has been planning its lifetime for months or even years. Although in a baby, this is an adult soul, with wisdom and knowledge, desires and goals, that has just entered this world to begin an incarnation. There is a lot of anticipation in the soul regarding the journey it has begun. Most souls are reuniting with families they've been with in other lifetimes. Most (but not all!) souls are looking forward to seeing old friends again and being back on earth. So much more is going on than just a baby being born.

As with everything, coming back to earth has a process to it. The process of coming into a body, or incarnating, is gradual. The soul needs time to adjust and is in and out of the body a great deal in the early years of childhood, which is why little ones sleep so much. Yes, we do need to work with these young beings; they need our guidance in learning to function on earth, but they are far from being empty shells.

I have been fortunate to be in the delivery room with at least ten women. I have also done many readings over the years for pregnant women who wanted psychic information on the babies they were carrying. These experiences have taught me a lot about the soul, the body, and the birth process. In the next chapter we'll take a look at life through the eyes of a soul. In this chapter we'll focus specifically on birth because that's where we assume our journey begins.

The soul is connected to its new body throughout the pregnancy, yet spends most of its time on the other side continuously preparing for its new life. The soul frequently visits its prospective parents, siblings, and environment throughout the pregnancy and usually enters the body at birth or directly after. Sometimes, if the baby is having a difficult time being born, the soul will enter the body before birth to help its body out of the birth canal. Most souls prefer to wait until their bodies are born for two reasons: because birth is painful, and because this is an adult soul entering a tiny body — it's cramped in there!

I recently gave a talk about life, death, and life after death. During the talk I covered the subject of birth and shared with the audience stories about the souls I have seen in the delivery room. It is amazing to watch these souls anticipating their births and waiting to enter their new bodies. After the lecture a woman approached. She was an obstetrician. She thanked me and said that she would never look at her work in quite the same way because she had never given any thought to what the soul might be doing during a birth. This information had given her a whole new perspective.

Timing

We are always anxious to have the baby born, especially in that ninth month when mom is so uncomfortable. She can't sit, walk, sleep, breathe, or do much of anything without feeling worn out. Relatives and loved ones call frequently to see if "anything's happening yet." The boss wants to know how soon she can go back to work. Baby showers, the nursery, the crib, bottles, diapers — everything is ready to go. Doctor visits are every week. Day turns into night. Night turns into day. The question on everyone's minds is, When is the baby coming? So much emphasis is put on one small aspect of birth.

There is much folklore and many old wives tales about how to start labor: vacuum the carpet, make love, run up and down the stairs, eat Chinese food, take hot baths, ride a bike, drink strange concoctions. I could go on and on, and yet I have seen in my work that none of this matters! The soul comes when the soul is ready and not before. As much as we like to think we have control over a baby's arrival, the bottom line is that the baby (the body) is born when the soul is ready. Overdue babies have souls that are not anxious to arrive any too soon. Premature babies have souls that are anxious and arrive early; other babies arrive on time because their souls are ready. If labor is induced or a C-section is performed, the soul comes in when it has to.

My son is a wonderful example. My due date was October 6. On October 13, I went into labor and dilated to four centimeters. My labor stopped and the doctor sent me home saying I would be back by the end of the day. Five weeks later, on November 20, my son was born — and that was only after being induced. Yes, I was as big as a house, but no matter what the doctor or I tried, he did not come until he was forced to. His personality today is strong willed; he doesn't want to be pushed into anything. He has definite ideas about life and the timing of things, and he likes doing things on his own terms and only when he is ready. So it would make sense that his soul would come in according to his agenda and not someone else's.

I had a client who came for a psychic reading on her unborn son. One of her questions was how the labor and delivery would go. She also wanted to know about the baby's personality. I opened psychically and could see his soul on the other side — he was reading! Several books were stacked in front of him, and he was in no hurry to get here. He told me that after he arrived, he was going to stay for a long time. He had not been on earth for generations and was reading up to prepare himself. He told me that he was a quiet sort of fellow and intended to remain so. He knew his new brother was somewhat ambivalent about his arrival, and he wished to reassure everyone that he would not be a problem. He asked me to tell his mother not to worry that she hadn't married his father, that she would be meeting someone new, and that he preferred this man as a parent.

When I asked about the labor and delivery, he gave me an odd look and told me it would not be easy. He would to be large and would not be coming until he absolutely had to. He was happy with life on the other side and was not necessarily looking forward to this incarnation. He, however, knew that after he arrived his memory of the other side would fade, and in time he would be fine with his life.

He ended up being four weeks overdue. The doctors gave his mother several medications over a three-week period to induce labor, and nothing happened. It's been several years now since his birth, and his mother tells me his personality is exactly as I had described in the reading.

I mentioned my good fortune at being present during several births. In most cases the soul was standing in the delivery room waiting for its body to enter the world. Twice I saw the soul standing with one or two guardian angels, discussing things. I couldn't hear the conversations, but in one case I did hear the soul say to its angel just before entering its body, "Keep me on track."

In a few deliveries, the soul didn't wait in the delivery room, but came flying into the room and entered its body immediately after birth. In two or three more difficult labor situations, I saw the soul go into the mother to help bring out the baby. Shortly before my nephew was born, the nurse checked my sister-in-law and told her it would be a while before she was ready to deliver, because she was only minimally dilated. I held my hands on her stomach and channeled healing energy to her, hoping to help the process be less painful. Out of nowhere I heard a voice say, "Look out!" — and a male soul rushed past me and literally dived into her stomach. Her body jolted, and she asked me to get the nurse right away because she could feel something had shifted. The nurse said there was no way the baby was coming soon, but I asked if she would please check again anyway because something had shifted in my sister-in-law's body. The nurse came back, and to everyone's great surprise she was almost ready to deliver. Within a half hour Blakey was born.

An interesting thing happened shortly afterward. Blakey cried inconsolably for some time, and nothing we did would calm him. The nurse took him to the nursery so my sister-in-law could get some sleep. I had the thought to communicate with his soul and find out what he needed. I went to the nursery and stood at the window. My spirit guide John appeared and said, "Call him Daniel because that was the name his soul was used to." Telepathically I sent a thought to the baby — I called him Daniel — and asked how I could help. The message came back that he was frightened to be in the world and wanted to go back. Then my guide told me he just needed to cry it out and that he would be all right as time passed. I think the little guy cried for a good hour before he finally fell asleep. In the weeks after his birth, whenever I held him I would look into his eyes, call him Daniel, and welcome him to his new life. His intense little eyes would stare deeply into mine as if to thank me for acknowledging him.

Infant Death, Abortion, and Miscarriage

When we try to understand the soul's view of birth, it makes sense that we take a look at miscarriage, abortion, and infant death. Sometimes, the soul is involved in these events. It's important to know, however, that the soul usually has quite a different perspective than we do. The following should help to illustrate.

A friend's nephew was born handicapped and died shortly afterward. My friend asked me what happens to the soul in that kind of situation. She wondered if the soul dies, also. I told her that souls don't die, and I opened psychically to get a read on the case. I saw the soul that was meant for that baby and asked him to explain what had happened. He told me that although he wanted to be in this family, he also wanted an athletic body and, because he was not in a hurry, would wait for a healthy body to house him. He said he felt bad for the family knowing their pain and loss, but to him the only loss was a defective physical form. I asked if he was attending the funeral and he said no, he felt no connection to the body. He also said that he would still be coming into this family and would simply wait for the mother to become pregnant again. Shortly afterward, my friend moved out of town and I did not keep in touch. I trust, however, that the soul did, in fact, come through this family.

I have been told that when a soul chooses a family and comes into a body it is given one year to decide if this is a "fit." It has to do with the soul's readiness to take on an incarnation. If the soul does not feel ready, it leaves the body and goes back to the other side to wait for better timing. This decision is what we call Sudden Infant Death Syndrome. It's no one's fault that the death of the physical body occurred. The soul simply was not ready. It will wait for the woman to become pregnant again. If the woman does not become pregnant, the soul will search for another family that will best suit its needs.

Abortion is one of those topics that most people would rather not discuss, but in just about every talk I've given, the subject comes up. People want to know what the soul's perspective is. What's most important to know about abortion is that it does not destroy a soul. If the woman chooses an abortion, it can be frustrating for a soul who wants to come through a specific woman or to a certain family because it either stops the soul from being born into that family or it makes the soul wait for her to become pregnant again.

Not all pregnancies are meant to go full term. Not all pregnancies have a soul assigned to them. In many abortion situations no soul was intended for that body, but there was something important in the experience for that woman, man, family, medical staff, town, and so on. It could be karmic, which simply means that because of some experience around pregnancy or abortion in a past life, this person needs to have this experience in this life. One example could be that the person may have been judgmental of abortion in a previous life and needs to experience it firsthand to gain empathy or compassion at a soul level. I've had numerous women come for psychic readings on whether or not to have an abortion. Instead of making the decision for them, the guides usually tell the women that if they feel emotionally attached to the pregnancy, probably a soul is assigned to the body and it's probably working very hard to convince her to carry full term. If the woman feels detached from the pregnancy, it could be one of those situations in which no soul is intended for that body, but the experience is an important one for the people involved.

I have done readings for a few clients when the circumstances were uncommon, but important to mention. Some clients came for healing a deep emotional pain stemming from a fear of being destroyed or unwanted; they never felt safe. No matter how much therapy they did, they couldn't bring up any memories to explain these feelings. In every case I've had a psychic image that their mothers had unsuccessfully tried to abort them. The memory was stored in their bodies. Because they were fetuses, there were no words to explain the terror. Their bodies also absorbed a lot of their mothers' feelings of fear, confusion, trauma, and anxiety, and they grew up with those feelings at their core. Even though the souls had not yet attached themselves to the bodies, the bodies retained the memories and were affected throughout their lifetimes.

I've also encountered women who have had abortions and the souls attached themselves to the woman in spite of their decision to abort. Those souls wanted to be born to one person so specifically that when the woman aborted, the soul decided to be with her anyway. The woman's conscious mind was not aware of the attachment, but *her* soul was aware and knew she was taking care of the other soul. If I hadn't seen it with my own eyes I wouldn't have believed it; however, I have seen it in a few cases. What was interesting to me was that when I told each woman about the attached soul, none was surprised. Each expressed having a feeling of mothering *something* on a different level, but didn't understand what it meant.

There is one last piece about abortion I would like to add. If you've had an abortion and are now having trouble getting pregnant, I strongly suggest doing some grief and forgiveness work about the abortion. Many women have come to me for healing regarding infertility problems, and when I look inside psychically, I see a "shadow" of a baby inside the uterus. It's as if that loss was never fully grieved and its shadow still sits inside the womb, leaving no room for a new fetus to grow. For us to continually move forward in life, it's very important to heal all our old pain and trauma.

I've done several readings for women who have suffered the experience of a miscarriage, and I've seen a variety of reasons why the miscarriage may have happened:

- There may have been something wrong with the fetus.

- The soul coming in wanted a different sex than was originally created.

- The timing wasn't right for the soul coming in.

- The timing wasn't right for the mother.

- There was no soul intended for the pregnancy, so the body released the fetus.

- It was a life (karmic) experience the mother's soul chose to have.

Just as with abortion, when a woman miscarries, and a soul was waiting to be born into that family, it will wait for the woman to become pregnant again. If pregnancy does not occur, the soul will find another family.

It's important to note here that I have done psychic readings on only a tiny percentage of all the women who have lost babies through infant death, have had abortions, or have had miscarriages. I can only assume that these reasons are not all the explanations, but rather are some of the most common reasons.

Happy Birthday

I would like to end this chapter with a great story that taught me something special about birthdays.

My friend Valerie started her consistent labor pains about 7:00 P.M. We left for the hospital around 3:30 A.M. when her contractions were about three minutes apart. It was her first baby, so we figured we had plenty of time. When we got to the hospital, the nurse told her she had barely dilated, so we knew we were in for a long wait. I started channeling healing to help her body open for the birth. About noon the nurse suggested I get some food while Val tried to sleep. In the cafeteria I was sitting in a sleepy daze looking out at the cold, snowy day when I thought to ask my guides what was taking so long. Suddenly Val's deceased grandmother appeared to me. She told me that Valerie was afraid to open her heart to this baby because she had been hurt so much. She told me to reassure Val that she would make a good mother and not to worry about not being able to provide for her child. She said to tell Val to ask God for help in opening her heart to the baby.

When I asked her grandmother where the soul of the baby was, she said he was at a birthday-going away party on the other side. She showed me an image of an adult male soul attending a party, celebrating and saying good-bye. I asked if this was common and she said yes, souls preparing to come back to earth have many friends and loved ones they will be leaving, so it is common to have some kind of celebration before they go. I asked her what time he would be arriving and she said at 8:30 that night. I thought, Oh my God, that's eight hours away — can't you talk him into coming earlier? But then it dawned on me that everything was in perfect order. The soul needed to go through his process of saying good-bye, and Val needed to go through her process of opening and welcoming the baby.

When I went back to the room, I told Val everything her grandmother had said, except the part about his arriving at 8:30. I didn't want her to feel discouraged.

She had a long, difficult labor, but did a great job. It was about 7:00 when she was fully dilated and ready to start pushing. An hour and a half later, the midwife told Val that the baby was stuck and she needed to call the doctor.

Just then I felt a rush of air and a presence come into the room. I looked across at Val and there was the soul I had seen earlier, standing at the head of the bed. He was tall, dark haired, dark eyed — he looked very much like his father.

I communicated with him telepathically and let him know his body was stuck. He told me that he knew. The nurse came into the room and said something to me about the doctor. I had looked away only for a second, but when I turned back, the soul was gone. My first thought was, "Great time to leave" — but within seconds, Val could feel something happening, and it occurred to me that maybe he had gone inside his body to help deliver it. At that point the midwife came into the room and within minutes we were holding a beautiful little baby boy named Micah. No C-section, no forceps, and Valerie was doing fine. The baby was extremely alert after birth, his eyes wide open. He looked at each of us as if to say, "Hello everyone, I'm back."

One final thought: I have worked with lots of individuals who were pregnant and also with many who were dying. In both cases the big question is how to speed the process, how to get that baby to come quicker or how to exit the world faster. Whether it's birth or death, the soul has its own timing and no matter what we do, we can't rush the process. It happens when the soul is ready to be released, either from life on the other side or life on this side.

We need to honor the wisdom of the soul, its timing, its agenda, and its process.

Chapter 4

Life: The School Called Earth

*It is not true that life is one damned
thing after another — it is one damn thing over and over.*

— Edna St. Vincent Millay

When our souls think about coming back to earth, returning to life in a body, they are thinking that it's time to go back to school. We were created with unlimited potential, and our responsibility as creations of God is to become the best we can be. The end result of all our lives, of all our learning, is to know our oneness with God, to love ourselves unconditionally, and to live whatever way we choose on the other side. To be in that place, we need to have the same understanding, knowledge, wisdom, and compassion that God has, and we attain that by having a vast range of experiences.

You've probably heard the expression "spiritually enlightened." What this expression means is that a person who has lived many lifetimes finally "gets it." This person knows that he or she is here to gain wisdom. Life isn't just a one-time experience. We can't possibly reach our highest potential in one lifetime. We reach that desired state of perfection by coming back life after life and having as many learning experiences as possible.

Planning Our Schooling — Reincarnation

When our souls feel the inner nudging that it is time to go back to school, they ask for help from the Elders. There are many names for these souls (such as oversouls), but my spirit guides call them "Elders." They are a group of wise, highly developed souls that help our souls plan each lifetime.

There is a place on the other side called the Akashic Hall of Records. When it is time to plan a life, the soul goes with the Elders to the hall and reviews its records. I always think of the records like big journals with all past lives recorded in them. The souls goes through its "journal" to see what is unfinished. What lessons does it need or want? What people does it have unfinished business with? What new skills does it want to acquire? These questions help plan its "schooling." A great deal of time and effort goes into the planning of each life so that the soul gets the most out of it. If it is an advanced or older soul, it can be part of the planning process. If it is relatively new, its life will be planned by the Elders.

If we think of the lessons chosen as classes in "earth school," here are some classes the soul may sign up for:

- Living in a functional or dysfunctional family

- Learning how to give or receive love, or both

- Making amends to those we have harmed in past lives

- Learning to communicate

- Learning about money, through either wealth or poverty

- Getting an education

- Having a career or job

- Being a certain religion, race, or color

- Experiencing gifts, talents, creativity, musical abilities

- Overcoming shortcomings

- Confronting fears

- Dealing with addictions, health challenges, weight issues, fame, marriage, divorce, heterosexuality, homosexuality

- Being mentally, emotionally, or physically challenged

- Parenting

- Fighting for a cause

- Helping to raise the consciousness of the planet

- Healing low self-worth

- Dealing with codependency issues, control issues

- Breaking abusive cycles

- Learning to experience happiness

After the soul chooses the experiences it wants to have, it chooses (or has chosen) a family that will help facilitate those lessons. Souls often come back to the same family system, which explains why even though you are the daughter in this lifetime, you feel like the mother or the father, or maybe why you've always thought of your brother as your father. Souls come back over and over with the same family, changing roles, walking in another's shoes if necessary, until all amends are made. Resentments, anger, and hatred are all healed. Then they move on to another family system.

Any unfinished business a soul has with someone from a past life must be finished. If the soul has resentments or hatred toward another person, it will keep coming back with that person until everything is worked out or until it forgives that person and itself for the situation(s) that caused those feelings.

Souls all have many lifetimes, living half their lifetimes as a male and half as a female in order to find God's perfect balance. Buddha said his soul had 550 lifetimes before he became the Buddha. Souls can't possibly gain all the wisdom available in just one life. They live in many situations to gain as much knowledge and understanding as they can.

Reincarnation, then, means to return again after death to the physical world in another body. Along with the learning and growing we do each lifetime, we are also balancing past karma. Karma means compensation. Jesus said, "As ye sow, so shall ye reap," meaning whatever we do unto others, whether it's positive or negative, will come back to us. If we have done something negative or hurtful to another person, we are held responsible for that action. I was curious about what the major religions believe about reincarnation, so I read Manly P. Hall's *Reincarnation: The Cycle of Necessity.* According to his research, Hinduism, Buddhism, ancient Judaism, and early Christianity believe in reincarnation, but current schools of Christianity and Islam do not.

Reincarnation logically explains so many things about life that otherwise remain mysterious:

- Why some are born healthy while others are born deformed, handicapped, or sick

- Why some are born rich and others live in poverty

- Why some parents lose their children early in life and others don't

- Why some are born with beauty and others not

- Why some are born extremely gifted, like the six year old who can compose a symphony or the three year old who understands math

- Why some have only one parent and others have multiple parents

- Why the divorce rate is so high

- Why racism exists and what it is all about

- Why we meet people we are immediately afraid of or we are instantly attracted to

- Why parts of the world seem familiar to us yet we've never been there before (in this lifetime)

- Why we have certain fears or abilities

- Why we have an understanding of certain races or religions without having lived them (to our knowledge)

- Why children speak in other languages or of other parents, homes, or names they had, or of events that took place in other lives

A story told to me by Pat, my three-year-old stepson, several years ago illustrates this final point quite nicely. We were going to visit my sister in the hospital. Pat asked me if she was going to die, which kind of surprised me, but I simply told him no, she was not going to die. Then he looked over at me and said, "Do you remember when I died?" I asked him what he meant and he said, "Don't you remember, my face was down in the dirt and I got scorched by the sun. You and my mom and dad were all there, don't you remember?" I told him that I couldn't remember and asked him what else he remembered, but he said that was all. I was blown away for a couple of reasons: one, because the word *scorched* seemed like such a big word for a three-year-old, and second because I always, ever since I had met his father, had the fear that he would die in my care. I didn't know that the thing I feared had already happened in a past life. The memory wasn't coming through to my conscious mind that clearly, but the feelings remained.

I was really grateful Pat shared this story with me because it also helped heal a tumultuous relationship between his mother and me. When I told her what Pat had said, she explained that she, too, had a fear that he was going to die when he was with me. That is why she had tried to prevent visitations with us. All the fear finally made sense.

I've since found out that it is not uncommon for children up to the age of five and some as old as seven to recall past lives. *Children's Past Lives* by Carol Bowman is a very good book I highly recommend. She has some wonderful stories about children's past life recall.

Spirit Guides

When we come to earth we also have the help and encouragement of our spirit guides. Everyone has guides. Some have the same guides throughout their lives, others have guides that change whenever a major event occurs in their lives. Souls that are allowed to be guides are usually more evolved. They're not judgmental or negative. They're in our lives to be of positive help on our path. Guides may be friends of our souls who have agreed to be guides in this lifetime and help keep us on track according to what we came here to do. They speak to us through our thoughts, our feelings, our dreams. They speak to our souls daily.

Our guides may also be angels. Angels are the sweetest group of beings I've ever encountered. They are filled with joy and enthusiasm and love, and they help us out as much as they can. They protect us, help us stay on our path, stand by us through tough times, and always somehow remain cheerful about it. I've also seen angels who are living here on earth in bodies. They've incarnated into bodies with the sole purpose of bringing more positive light and inspiration to the world.

You can usually tell when you've encountered an angel on earth because they are very loving, usually quite gentle, and they always have a positive outlook on everything. If I hadn't seen wings on some of the "earth angels" I've encountered, I never would have believed it's true.

Even though you may not be conscious of spirit guides and angels working with you, they are still there, communicating with your soul whenever they need to.

If you would like to become more familiar with your guides, simply tell them daily that you would like to get to know them more consciously. Talk to them as if they are right there with you (they are). Just as with any relationship, you need to work at developing a relationship with your guides by putting some daily effort into it. Ask them to help you know when they're around. It takes time to establish a conscious relationship with them because they don't have the same means to communicate as you do, but they will do their best to make contact.

Past Life Issues

I'd like to give you some examples of how souls choose to work out issues they have from previous lives. We are always trying to figure out why we go through some of the experiences we have, but often our experiences are not happening for the reasons we consciously think they are. Many of us believe our life challenges are coming from God, but the truth is that many are simply our soul's way to heal issues. From our limited point of view, it may seem like certain issues aren't fully resolved. As the guides have said, it's best not to judge ourselves. The best approach to take with any experience is to accept that there is a valid reason for having it (from our soul's point of view) and learn as much from the experience as we can. Our experiences are for our soul's benefit, not for ours.

Conscientious Objector

John was a client who had a terrible feeling about the Vietnam war and had felt very strongly that he should not go. As a conscientious objector, he had moved to Canada to avoid the draft. This had bothered him a great deal, but he had felt strongly that he could not have gone to fight. He came for a reading because he wanted to come to terms with his refusal to fight for his country. I saw in the reading that he had died twice while fighting in wars, and his soul was determined not to have life taken again at an early age. It was not part of the plan for this lifetime.

After hearing this information, John felt very relieved to know there were valid reasons for his current values.

Letting Go

Betsy at age three started telling her mother that she was going to be a doctor. That was all she had thought about while growing up. She had entered medical school, but after a short time felt very disappointed, and she wanted to find something completely different to do. She came to me for a psychic reading and had two main questions: Why had she totally lost interest in her lifelong dream and what was she supposed to do now?

What came up in the reading was an image of her as a physician in a previous life. She identified so strongly with being a doctor that her soul would not let it go. The guides told her to find something other than the medical field because she was not meant to be a doctor again, to stop pressuring herself because it was good she had changed her strong opinion about medical school. They wanted her to move on and find something she really wanted to do versus what she felt she should do. She appeared relieved by the information, and although I didn't hear from her again I feel confident she was able to move on.

Sexual Preference

Cliff came to me for a reading about his homosexuality. He wondered why God made him gay. He wanted to know what he had done in a past life to deserve it, because being gay was difficult for him.

In the reading the guides said that Cliff's soul had just finished several lifetimes in succession as a female and had been told by the Elders to start balancing himself, to start developing more of the male side. For this lifetime they chose a male body for him. They said he had not done anything wrong and the homosexuality was not meant as a punishment. They told him the reason for his sexual preference was that to his soul it felt more natural to be with a man than with a woman. They said it would take one more lifetime for his soul to really embrace his male energy, but that he was moving toward being a more balanced soul.

I have seen similar situations with women who are trying to understand their lesbianism. Their souls have lived several lives in succession as men and now need to start balancing themselves. One lesbian client asked if my guides thought she was disgusting because of her sexuality, and my guides were quite surprised at that question. Guides don't make judgments about anyone's sexual preference. They see everything as an experience the soul chooses.

I did a reading on Hal, another homosexual client, who was told in the reading that the reason he was gay in this lifetime was karmic. In a previous life, he had been extremely judgmental toward homosexuals and would make their lives miserable whenever he had a chance. The guides said his soul needed to walk in the shoes of a gay man and find out what it was like, thus giving up judgments. This is how the soul was to balance his karma.

Hal wasn't surprised to hear this, because even though he was gay, another part of him was very critical of homosexuals. He said that it was difficult for him to think of himself as "one of them" and always kept himself separate. The guides suggested he open his heart to himself as well as to other gay people, get to know them, and begin his healing process. Hal told me he would work on it, but I never saw him again.

An Incestuous Relationship

A young woman named Carrie was an incest victim, and she wanted to know, first of all, why — and second, why she enjoyed it. She felt very ashamed of this and had told almost no one. Although the incest had ended, she really missed the relationship with her father and wondered if the key to understanding it could be in a past life.

I was very curious to see what the guides would say, and when they gave me the answer it almost seemed too easy. Carrie and her father had been lovers in a past life. It was that simple. They came into this lifetime together hoping to take the relationship to another level. They had experienced so much more together as father and daughter, but still had a sexually involved relationship. Carrie said it had been years since they were sexual. Her father had moved out of town to get away from her, and the sexual part of their relationship had stopped. She still missed it, even after ten years. The guides said that perhaps in a future life they would choose to be lovers again, but for this lifetime they were to concentrate on being father and daughter and to take the sexuality out of their relationship.

Carrie came for two more healings to help heal the grief she felt around the loss of her relationship with her father. The last time I saw her, she said that her relationship with her husband was becoming more fulfilling as she continued to work on closing the door to her father and opening to more intimacy with her husband. She said that knowing she and her father had been lovers helped heal a lot of the shame she carried throughout her life.

Racial Preference

Estelle came for a reading to understand why she was attracted only to black men. She said it wasn't a problem for her as much as it was for her parents and friends, who were all from a small town. She preferred African-American food, music, dance, and the entire culture, and she even felt black in some way, although obviously she wasn't. You can probably guess the psychic information that came through:

Estelle's soul had been black in several lives and wanted to come again as a black person. The Elders told her soul that she needed to experience the white culture because in the past she had been quite judgmental toward whites.

When I told her, she laughed and told me she still had that attitude, that for as long as she could remember she had not trusted white people and felt safe only around black people. The guides strongly suggested she try to understand the culture of her birth. She needed to focus on healing the resentments she held toward the white race.

Estelle came for several healings to help her in the process. She had numerous issues around mistrust that needed to be addressed and healed for her to feel more whole. Several events took place in Estelle's life during the time our healing sessions were going on that enabled her to open up and trust white people more. It was a fascinating process to watch — and today Estelle has family and friends in both cultures.

Fears of Enclosed Spaces and Darkness

Sarah was claustrophobic and afraid of the dark. She felt that as an adult she should have overcome these fears, and she shouldn't have to sleep with a light on.

In the reading I saw an image of Sarah's soul in an Egyptian lifetime buried alive after her tongue had been cut out. She was a man in that life and had lied about someone to protect himself. This caused the other person to be put to death. When the man was found out, he suffered this kind of death as a result. The guides told us that Sarah's soul still harbored terror and required healing. She needed to forgive herself and realize she had come a long way since that life. Sarah was told to ask God for help in healing the memories. While I channeled this information to her, she had a very difficult time breathing, so difficult that a couple of times I thought that maybe I should call an ambulance. She managed to get through it, and the next time I saw her she had worked through the feelings of terror with her therapist. Sarah was now sleeping with the lights off.

Fear of Fire

By working through a past life trauma, Lee came to understand her fear of fire. As a little girl her fear had been really bad, but it had calmed down as she got older. Recently, however, the fear had become very strong again, to the point where she smelled smoke all the time and was waking several times during the night to see if the house was on fire — even though there were smoke detectors she checked regularly.

The guides said that she was currently dating a man who has been her son in a previous life. During that incarnation Lee had been a woman who was a farmer, and her five-year-old son had set the farmhouse on fire, burning it to the ground and killing himself. The farmer had been absolutely devastated by the loss of both her house and child, and never fully regained herself in that lifetime. When Lee started to date her current boyfriend, all the old feelings locked deep in her soul surfaced once again. The guides explained that this was why she felt "clingy" toward this man and almost panicky every time he left, as though he might never return. Lee verified that these feeling were indeed the truth.

The guides suggested that she spend the next three days watching sad movies, specifically with themes of loss. They instructed her to really get into her emotions and work at letting them go. After this purge she would be free to build a new relationship with this man.

Lee called me the following day to say that she had shared with her boyfriend the information from the reading. He told her that when he was a little boy, he had a problem with starting fires. He had started the couch on fire and nearly burned down the family home! He told her that after he turned five his desire to start fires completely stopped.

Shortly after the reading, Lee and her boyfriend both felt a healing had taken place between them. They continued to date for a few months, but eventually split up. She told me they remained very good friends, but both felt a need to let go of the other.

Fear of Pregnancy

Molly came for a healing and reading regarding her fear of pregnancy. She said it was so strong that it was ruining her marriage because her husband really wanted children.

When I opened psychically I saw an image of her dying in childbirth in a former life. My guides said that Molly needed to sit and visualize dying while giving birth. She then needed to write all her feelings about it — just let all the thoughts and sensations flow from her body onto paper until she felt really done. They said it wouldn't be hard to access the feelings stuck in her soul because they were near the surface. That's why she felt the fear so intensely — it was no longer buried deep within. Molly was choosing to heal this fear now so she could have children in this lifetime. Molly reported back about a year later to tell me she had followed the guides' suggestions and her fears had lifted. She had just given birth to a baby girl.

I can't tell you the number of women I have seen with this kind of trauma. Fear of pregnancy or of giving birth is fairly common, and the fear can be so intense that it can actually prevent pregnancy or cause all kinds of female reproductive problems, including infertility.

Hypnotists who do past life regressions have found that unresolved emotions from our past lives are continually affecting us. In my work, I have seen this with all kinds of fears, such as fear of fire, water, heights, dogs, horses or other animals, knives, swords or other sharp objects, darkness, certain races or groups of people, and specific places and times in history. When we have had an experience in a past life that caused us emotional anguish and we haven't done anything with those feelings, they sit in our souls until we identify with them and begin a healing process to really own them and work through them.

Health Issues

Sylvia came for a reading and a healing on her physical condition. She had experienced health problems since childhood and was always at one specialist or another. They all seemed to have a different opinion of what was wrong with her. She had taken so many medications that she was immune to antibiotics and quite sensitive to many other drugs. She wanted to know where to go next, what kind of doctor to see.

Sylvia didn't necessarily believe in past lives, so when my guides immediately went into information about her past lives in the reading, she didn't pay much attention. She was more concerned with finding the person who could "fix" her. The guides said that in a past life she was a male doctor, but not a very reputable one. He spent almost no time listening to his patients and was quick to prescribe any kind of medication. As long as his patients thought he had done something to improve their health, he felt justified in charging large sums of money. In addition, he particularly disliked his female patients, thinking they were all just hysterical women who wanted attention. In this lifetime Sylvia was on the receiving end of this kind of treatment.

The guides also said that she needed to stop giving doctors so much power and realize she could listen to and care for her own body. She had a deep belief that doctors knew it all, and she needed to learn that this wasn't true. The guides said that her health was dependent on her viewing her health, and her health care, entirely differently. She needed to take her power back and stop giving it all to the medical profession. She needed to start taking responsibility for herself and to learn through meditation how to connect with her body and her body's wisdom about what it needs. They said not to exclude doctors, but not include any doctors who have the same attitude she had in that past life.

I don't think she heard a word I said. When she left she mentioned another specialist and said that maybe she should try him. I was glad I had taped the session, because I think that someday she may want to hear it again, and it will click with her and she'll get on track. If not, what will happen? She will have another life and go through similar experiences again. Unfortunately, the circumstances will probably intensify to get her attention before she finally learns to take responsibility for the state of her health.

Jackie had a similar situation, but the karma was completely different. She, too, had a lot of physical problems and had been to several doctors. They were not in agreement about what was wrong with her, and she developed allergies to several medications as well.

Jackie's approach to her session was entirely different. She wondered what she had done in a past life to bring this on. When was it going to stop? What could she do to help herself? The guides said that Jackie had been a nurse in a past life. She had been frustrated with the lack of authority in her position, for she continually took orders and did the jobs no one else wanted. They said that her soul wanted to be a doctor and decided first to have a life being sick to develop as much compassion as possible for what people go through. They told her that she would be an excellent doctor in a future life. She was then advised to explore spirituality and learn how to use it to cope with her physical problems.

Every time Jackie came for a healing, I could see that her soul was quite pleased with all that she was learning — although, from my human point of view, the experiences she was going through seemed pretty difficult. All her doctors had differing opinions; she was on several medications that caused physical problems. Her husband had no tolerance for illness, and her children were impatient with her slow progress. Even though consciously she was always feeling discouraged, her soul was always very happy about the knowledge she was gaining.

Her soul told me she looked forward to "graduating" — which she eventually did. After Jackie's death, her soul communicated with me that she was delighted with herself for all Jackie's courage and for all she had learned.

These stories bring up an important point about not judging ourselves or others for what we or they are going through. Life looks one way to us consciously — but our souls view it from a much higher perspective, always from an attitude of learning and growing from it.

Relationships

One client come for a healing on her back. Karen had been to several doctors to find the cause of her back pain. No one could find anything wrong. She asked if I could see what the pain was about and suggest how to get rid of it. The guides showed me an image of Karen as a man on horseback wearing a suit of armor. He looked as if he was getting ready to go into battle. Then another man came from behind and thrust a sword into his back, killing him. The guides explained that the two men were battling over the love of a young woman, that the man who had murdered Karen was currently her fiancé, and that her back started to hurt when he came into her life. The young woman they had fought over was now her fiancé's daughter from a previous marriage.

Karen found this information remarkable for two reasons: one, she said that she and her fiancé were always fighting about his daughter and, two, she always felt a need to watch her back when he was around, but she had no idea why.

I saw her several months later, and she told me she was no longer engaged. She said they had remained good friends after they were honest with each other about their feelings, but they had both realized they didn't want to get married. They made amends for all the hurtful things they had done to each other in the relationship, and it was at that point that the pain in her back stopped. The old wounds were healed.

Another client wanted to understand her relationship with her father. All her life Renee had felt it was her job to take care of him. She felt guilty for wanting to move away and for not being there when he needed her. They had an emotionally incestuous relationship. She had been in therapy for quite a while, but was not having much luck in making a change.

When I looked at it psychically, I got an image of a Native American woman who was pregnant. I saw her walk into the woods, squat by a tree, and give birth to a baby boy, then walk away, crying all the way back to her village. I asked my guides why Renee left the baby by the tree, and they said that she was not married and didn't feel able to care for the child. She felt terrible; she wanted to keep the baby, but saw no way to do so without embarrassing herself, her family, and the man who had fathered the child. The guides said the baby boy was now her father, and she had promised not to abandon him again. Renee was still carrying guilt from that past life and needed to forgive herself.

The guides suggested that she write out all the feelings she had about the responsibility she felt to her father, and then she could stop taking care of him and move on. After the reading Renee shared with me that her father had been adopted and that he loved to focus on the fact that he had been "abandoned" by his birth mother. Obviously there was something his soul needed to go through relating to the issue of abandonment.

I saw Renee about a year later, and she was doing much better. She said that after her reading it took a while for her to let her father go. She joined a twelve-step group that taught detachment and letting go. She worked with her therapist to release the guilt she felt, and slowly, over time, felt the old feelings healing. She felt much freer, although her father was still struggling with his neediness and fear of abandonment.

Addictions and Codependency

Many people have asked me why a soul would choose alcoholism or drug addiction as a life lesson. Some may have to go through it because they were judgmental of alcoholics in a past life and need to come back and experience it themselves. I have seen several souls who have destroyed their bodies in past lives because of substance abuse. They then have to keep coming back until they stop the self-destructive cycle and break their addiction. I have seen other souls who simply want to have the experience of drug or alcohol dependency.

Codependency is another interesting life lesson. Some people are so enmeshed, so dependent on others, that they are continually stuck in a cycle of self-loss. They have little or no self-worth and must take care of others to feel good about themselves. Codependents need to break that cycle and learn how to take care of themselves. They have to realize that they are not being selfish, but rather self-honoring. All of us eventually need to get to the place where we are focusing on ourselves, helping ourselves, healing ourselves, making ourselves whole rather than focusing on others and what they need to the exclusion of ourselves. We are all responsible for our own well-being, and to suffer from codependency takes us away from ourselves in an unhealthy way. To reach the highest state of perfection, we need to know self-love, and codependency is the opposite of self-love.

Thoughts on Karma

One of Jesus' teachings was to love thy neighbor as thyself. Many of us still believe it is more honorable to love thy neighbor and forget about ourselves, but that is not the way it goes. We have to love and honor ourselves as much as God does! And if we aren't, we keep coming back until we do. Some of you may think that the karmic stories in this chapter sound pretty intense; others may think they are easy compared to what they've experienced in this life. Depending on what you came into this lifetime to achieve, you may have returned for one life lesson or you may have signed on for twenty, thirty, or forty life lessons — all in this one life! It is not unreasonable for us to have experienced most of the issues in just one lifetime. If so, your soul may be in a hurry to work out all its "stuff." Remember, the soul's goal is to be done with life here and move up to higher and higher levels on the other side.

Here's a very important thing to realize: We are not meant to float through life as victims of our circumstances. We have a great deal to do with our lives and how they turn out, how we turn out. We can make the most of life, and even enjoy it, or we can fight it and focus on how awful it is. There are choices to be made every day as to how we are going to perceive and live our lives. We are not here by accident, and there are no coincidences. We need to pay attention. The fact that we are here is important. We're all here to grow and to become the best and most loving we can be.

When we complete our lessons here on earth, our souls want to be on their way. They want to graduate, which is what we call physical death. Our souls have worked hard, and even though our lives sometimes may not make sense on a conscious level, subconsciously our souls are delighted with the wisdom that was gained.

Chapter 5

Death: Graduation

It is impossible that anything so natural, so necessary and so universal as death, should ever have been designed by Providence as an evil to mankind.

— Jonathan Swift

Death. Hearses, caskets, wakes, Shiva, funerals, flowers, graveyards, crematoriums, black clothes, mourning, urns, memorial services, obituaries, widows, tombs, twenty-one-gun salutes, grieving, emptiness, loss, loneliness, sympathy cards, *pain*. It's really unfortunate how much pain and suffering we experience around death. There is no greater loss for those of us on this side of the veil when someone we love dies — and yet for those crossing over, it's graduation day.

Several years ago a close friend of mine lost her son in an accident. With my physical eyes I watched what his family was going through, and through my psychic eyes I saw what the young boy's soul was going through. It was an amazing experience, and I feel very grateful to have been a part of it.

My friend Maureen had received a phone call from the local hospital asking her to come immediately because her son, Jason, had been in an accident. She had no idea what condition he was in when the nurse called, and asked if I would meet her there.

When I arrived at the hospital, a nurse met me at the elevator and explained that early tests indicated there was little, if any, function in Jason's brain and that the prognosis was bleak. She asked if I would try to help Maureen understand the seriousness of her son's condition.

When I entered Jason's room, I could tell by the expression on everyone's face this was a very serious situation. His body lay very still and was hooked up to several machines. Maureen was understandably distraught and asked me to please channel spiritual healing to him.

As soon as the medical team cleared out of the room and I was alone with him, I laid my hands on his chest. I intended to channel a healing to him, but no energy came out of my hands. I opened psychically to communicate with his soul. I expected to find it inside his body or at least in the room, but instead I saw a very clear image of his soul on the other side, walking with two guardian angels. I also saw his deceased grandparents standing nearby. I called out his name psychically and asked if he could explain what was happening with his body and what his soul was doing on the other side. He looked at the two angels and told me they were just explaining that he was going to stay with them. Jason's grandfather told me he and his grandmother would be taking care of him.

I was stunned. I asked if this meant he was really going to die, and the grandfather said, very peacefully, "Yes, this is the day he is going to die." I was in shock. Three days earlier he had celebrated his twelfth birthday — and here he was today, calmly getting ready to let go of his young life. I asked his soul if there was anything I could do for him, and he asked me to find his father and get him to the hospital before he died.

Then the picture of Jason on the other side went blank, and my spirit guides told me not to pull on him with questions. Even though he appeared calm, he was in a state of confusion. They asked me to work with his parents to help them accept what was happening to their young son.

I walked out of the room and down the hall. I needed some air and time to digest all of this. The human part of me was having a tough time accepting that he was going to die. I didn't know what to tell his parents. I asked God to work with me each step of the way and help me to do what was right for everyone involved.

I asked Jason's sister where her father was, and she said he was in Mexico on vacation. No one knew how to reach him or when he would be back. Right after she said this, one of my spirit guides told me to call the airport and have him paged *now.* I called the terminal and had him paged. He picked up the phone within thirty seconds and told me that he was walking out the front door when he heard the page! I told him what was happening and he rushed directly to the hospital.

It was a grueling thirty hours from the time Maureen first got the phone call to the time they disconnected Jason from the life-support machines. I watched the unbearable pain his family and friends went through trying to accept his death, and at the same time saw the calmness in his soul as he moved on. I saw such love and comfort on the faces of those welcoming him to the other side.

Over the last thirty years as a spiritual healer, I have seen many similar situations with clients and their loved ones. Death is probably the toughest thing we humans have to deal with, and yet, from the standpoint of the soul, it is a transition that is perfectly natural, even welcome.

The Soul's Agenda

For His Highest Good

Recently I received a phone call from a doctor in California asking me to please send healing to her seventy-seven-year-old father who was in the hospital dying. He had several serious physical problems, but in spite of that she still wanted him to live. She said it would be really upsetting for the family if he died, and her mother might not survive the loss.

I told her that I have found over the years when praying for healing for someone who is very sick that the healing sometimes helps the person die. It can help the soul release from the body. She asked me to please focus on him living, not dying. I told her I would pray for healing for his highest good and that I would pray for healing for the rest of the family so that they could accept whatever the outcome was. I could hear in her voice the same ambivalence I hear in everyone's voice when I say those words. She didn't want to think about the possibility her loved one may die. To us living human beings, death is the enemy. We hate the word and loathe the feelings of loss. As far as we are concerned, there isn't one good thing about death unless it stops a loved one's suffering.

When I was first learning about the soul being in charge rather than our human body-mind, I didn't really like it — but the truth is, the journey here on earth is for our soul's development. The physical body is simply our covering, the vehicle we use to live out each incarnation. The body-mind is not in charge of key issues in our lives such as when to be born and when to die. The soul chooses when it's finished. In the father's case, he died shortly after I began praying for his highest good.

The Right to Decide

About twelve years ago my sister, Nikki, developed a rare lung disease called Hammond-Rich Syndrome. The doctors told us the disease was fatal and that she had a 50 percent chance of dying within two weeks of diagnosis. Our family was devastated. The doctor advised us not to tell her she had a deadly disease. She believed she had double pneumonia.

I started channeling healings to her right away, and, slowly we started seeing improvements. About two weeks into the healings she became very despondent. For three days she barely spoke to anyone and seemed distant and withdrawn. She wouldn't smile. It was as if her soul were not in her body. The doctor told us he was very concerned that she was getting worse. No matter what prayer I said or how much

I pleaded with God, no healing energy would come through my hands. On the third day I was very afraid Nikki was going to die. I couldn't accept what was going on. She was only twenty-nine years old and, from my perspective, had everything to live for.

I called my minister, and his wife told me it sounded like my sister's soul was in the process of making a decision whether or not to live. She told me I had to let her go and accept whatever decision her soul made. My first response was that I couldn't do that. I had to find a way to make my sister want to live. I paced back and forth all night, crying and talking to God. Finally, at four in the morning I stopped crying. I had finally gotten to a place where I was willing to accept whatever her soul wanted to do, although I certainly didn't feel good about it.

I slept briefly, got up early, and went to the hospital. When I opened the front door of the hospital, my hands started to heat with healing energy. When I got to Nikki's room, she was sitting up in bed, smiling. She said, "Well, let's get going on those healings, okay?" I knew that her soul had made the decision to stay. Weeks later, when she got out of the hospital, I told her what my minister's wife had said. She said she had no conscious recollection of making such a decision, in fact couldn't remember those three days at all. Her response to me was that of course she would choose to live; how silly of me to think otherwise!

Our bodies were created with a deep desire to survive. They don't want to die. They have an incredible tolerance for damage and destruction. I can think of alcoholic friends who existed on cheap wine, sterno, mouthwash, or whatever was available to get them high. They didn't waste money on nutritious food, worry about enough exercise, or get eight hours of sleep a night. They just drank, day after day, winter, spring, summer, and fall, and in spite of all the toxins they consumed, their bodies were determined to survive. I believe we live as long as we do because our souls have a need for our bodies, not because of the care we give to our bodies. The care we give our bodies determines the quality of life we'll have, but not the length of life.

From a psychic point of view I have seen over and over that the soul has one agenda and the body usually has another. Very seldom does the body know what the soul is up to because the soul doesn't want the conscious mind to interfere. It knows what it needs to accomplish, and the conscious mind may not understand.

Randy, a thirty-year-old female client, had lung cancer. She came for healings for three months, and she appeared to be getting better every time I saw her. One day she walked into my office looking very depressed. She had been to her doctor and was told she was getting worse and didn't have much longer to live. She wanted me to check with her soul to see what was going on.

During the healing I asked her soul if she would tell me what was happening. Her soul came out of the body and very happily informed me she would be "graduating" in two weeks. Her soul didn't want the body to know, however, because there were things to accomplish before leaving. She wanted to shop for a new dress, plant a perennial garden for her husband so that next spring the flowers would remind him of her, and have lunch with several friends. Then her soul would be ready to go. Again, her soul asked me not to tell the body; if her conscious mind knew that soon it was time to leave, her body-mind would sink into a depression and she would not get anything done.

I was really amazed by how different the two parts of her seemed. I told her that her soul didn't want to talk today, and she seemed relieved. She told me she wasn't going to believe the doctor, but was going to continue her healing sessions and continue to get better.

Two weeks later Randy's husband phoned to let me know she had made her transition. I asked him at the funeral how she had been doing before her death, and he told me she had been busy planting a garden, had spent time shopping for a new dress that she had on in the casket, and had seen several friends for lunch. He said she got worse suddenly and died. It was exactly the way her soul wanted it.

Another client, Martin, also had cancer. He came for a healing a few days before Christmas, and he emphatically told me he wanted to know if and when he was going to die. He said his family was waiting for him to come home with an answer! His soul, however, had a different agenda and just as emphatically stated that under no circumstances was I to tell the body that he was going to die in the spring. His soul said he had so much to accomplish before leaving and that he also wanted this to be a very special Christmas because it would the last one with his family. Martin's soul said that if his body went home and told his family that he would be dying in a few months, they would not enjoy their Christmas together. He said to tell his body that I could not get any information. Just like my other client, Martin seemed relieved to hear I didn't know when his death was coming.

Everybody's death process is different, and the reasons for that vary. Some have chosen to work out life lessons through their death process. Others are working on learning how to let go, surrendering. Others don't have life lessons left to work out, and their deaths are quick.

Over the years so many people have asked me why God makes people suffer in death. There are numerous reasons why our death process goes the way it does, and it isn't because God is punishing us, as some of us have been taught to believe. The stories in the rest of the chapter contain a variety of situations that have taught me about the death process.

Her Last Lifetime

One of my best friends died of lung cancer. JoAnn had always had a hard time receiving from others and prided herself on being totally independent, not needing anyone. Her death process took two years. I believe it took so long because her soul needed to learn how to receive from people. It needed to be dependent and vulnerable, and being sick for that length of time put her in a perfect position to experience those traits. Many times her soul told me this was going to be her last lifetime and she wanted to get it right so she wouldn't have to come back. I believe in those two years that is exactly what happened.

JoAnn had numerous experiences she would not otherwise have had while in a healthy body. She had to rely on others to drive her, do her shopping for her, help her get dressed and undressed, and eventually feed her. Near the end of her life, she lost her capacity to speak and had to rely on others to communicate for her. Every experience had to do with learning how to depend on others, how to be vulnerable and not in control.

My New Friend

I had an eighteen-year-old client who was dying from cancer. Amy had fought hard to live, but nothing was working. Her parents asked me if I would channel healing to her to help alleviate some of the pain. During the channeling, I asked her soul to tell me how she was *really* doing. I knew what the doctors were saying about her physically, but I wanted to know about her soul.

Amy's soul was angry — angry that she was dying at such a young age. She didn't want to leave family or friends and was especially concerned that everyone she knew was still in a body. Instead of trying to convince Amy's soul that she would be very happy on the other side, I decided just to let her soul talk and vent her feelings, because that's what her soul needed the most. Her soul thanked me for the healing and asked me to come back in about two weeks. I knew the healing would be to help her soul let go of her body, but neither of us mentioned it.

Two weeks later I did another healing. When I opened psychically to communicate with Amy's soul, she was quite different this time. Her soul was very happy, even bubbly, and she introduced me to her new friend, Mara, a young female spirit who had died of the same form of cancer Amy had. She told me her guides brought them together and that Mara had showed her around heaven, which she said was a "really cool place." She said now that she had a friend it wouldn't be so hard to go. She had seen movie stars there and there was a community of young people just like herself where she would live. Amy told me she would miss her family, especially her mom, and gave me a message to give to her. Then she thanked me for the healing and told me she would see me when I got to the other side. She graduated three days later.

The Machines Kept Him Stuck

A few years ago I went to the hospital with a friend to see his uncle, who was in a coma. When I went into his room, I saw his soul on the other side, mingling with friends and deceased family members, while his body remained alive only through the support of machines. My guides told me his soul was almost completely out of his body — his soul would be gone by the end of the day — but he needed the silver cord severed to be free. The life supports were keeping him trapped.

What I thought was interesting was how clever his soul was. His soul first came back into his body and appeared to improve physically. As a result, the doctors took him off some machines. After they did that, his soul was able to free himself from the body, and he died that night.

He Didn't Want to Hurt His Grandson

Thomas, a young man in his early thirties, called my office one day and asked if I would come to the hospital and do healings on his grandfather. Thomas said both his father and grandfather where in intensive care as the result of a car accident. His grandmother had been killed in the accident. As I drove to the hospital, I opened psychically to see what the situation would be like.

I could see that the grandfather's soul was barely attached to his body, and I knew he would be leaving soon. He felt stuck, however. The father felt quite different; his soul was still very attached to his body. I knew the father wouldn't be dying, but could see his rehabilitation would take a long time.

When I arrived Thomas was standing by the elevator, waiting to greet me. He looked scared. We went to his grandfather's room, and on the way he said several times that I had to heal his grandfather. He kept saying, "Please don't let my grandfather die. He's a really good man, and I love him a lot. I need him to live. Please don't let him die."

Thomas's grandfather was well into his eighties. I told Thomas I wanted to communicate with his grandfather's soul to see what he intended to do. His soul was not in his body, although the silver cord was still attached.

I could see his soul in the tunnel talking with a man. I called out his name and asked if he wanted me to channel healing to the body, and he said no. The soul said he was talking to his brother, the other man in the tunnel, about dying. The soul told me that he felt old, that the body was tired and in pain, that his brother was encouraging him to let go and come over to the other side. The soul said he wanted to be with his wife, but didn't want to hurt his grandson. The soul felt torn between doing what he wanted and doing what his grandson wanted, and asked if I would do a healing on his son, Thomas's father, who was down the hall. Then he turned away to talk with his brother.

I went to the other room to check on the father. He was in bad shape, with numerous broken bones. His jaw was wired shut and his body connected to several machines. Even though he was in a coma and appeared to be almost lifeless, his soul stood next to his body, very alert. His soul spoke to me and said he would gladly trade places with his dying father after his body was conscious and realized that he was responsible for his parents' deaths. Even though on a soul level this was how it was supposed to go, he didn't think he could go on living. He knew his family was very angry with him. He told me this was all karmic, and as much as he dreaded going through all of it, in about two years things would be a lot better. He spoke of two years as if it were two months. I asked if a healing would help. He laughed and said, "Where would you start?" Then he told me not to bother.

I went back to the grandfather's room and asked his soul if there was anything I could do to help. His soul was still in the tunnel with his brother, but turned to me and said he had made his decision and would be leaving in seventeen hours. He asked me to talk with his grandson and try to get him to understand that it was his time to go, that he needed to go.

I told Thomas that his grandfather would be leaving in seventeen hours and to spend as much time with him as possible and say everything he needed to say. I said that even though his grandfather's body appeared to be in a coma, his soul was fully conscious of everything that was happening. I called the next day to see how everyone was doing, and Thomas told me his grandfather died exactly seventeen hours after I had left.

The kind of struggle the grandfather experienced often happens when there is a strong emotional bond or when the dying person is codependent. Because codependents focus on what others want more than on what they want or need, the act of "dying" seems very selfish to them and they feel torn about what to do. That's why some people linger in death — they don't want to upset their loved ones.

He Didn't Want to Cause His Family Pain

Here's another story of a young man who had a similar kind of struggle. Matthew had been unconscious for months, and his family asked if I would come to the nursing home and communicate with his soul. They wanted to see what his soul needed to come out of the coma.

When I got to the room, I saw his soul standing at the side of the bed. He seemed to be having a very difficult time deciding whether to remain alive and go back into a body that was slowly deteriorating or make the final decision to let go and leave. His soul said he didn't want to hurt his family — they wanted him to live more than anything. They were an extremely loving family, and they came to visit him every day. Although his soul appreciated their caring, it was making it hard for him to go.

Matthew had suffered from a great many health problems all his life, and his soul was worn out. His soul told me he wanted to let go and go to the other side. He wished "someone higher up" would make the decision for him, but like the grandfather in the previous story, Matthew's soul needed to make the decision and take responsibility for his death.

Some souls really struggle with feeling selfish about this decision, especially when loved ones are begging and praying for them to live. I wasn't able to offer any help to Matthew, and I couldn't bring him out of the coma as his family wished. He lived another three weeks before letting go.

Let Me Do It My Own Way

This story is very special to me. Mark was just thirty years old and had a brain tumor. He was in the last stages of dying, and his wife asked if I could come to their home and channel healing to him because he was no longer able to come to my office. She said it felt as if he was stuck and had been lingering for so long. She asked if I would communicate with his soul and see what he needed in order to go on.

I visited Mark twice before he died. Each time I channeled a healing to him, his soul communicated to me. I wrote it down for his wife and, bless her heart, she gave me permission to share the notes with you. I'm including his soul's messages so that you can see the process he went through in letting go. Here are his soul's words to me five weeks before he died:

3/16/95

"I don't want to go anywhere. What if it isn't my time? What if I leave and then I realize I've made a mistake? What if my body bounces back? What if the tumor shrinks? What if I don't like it over there? What will my life be like without my wife, without my family? Why do I have to go first? Why is this happening to me? This isn't how it was supposed to go. I'm young. My body is strong."

He asked me if the healing was going to make him die, and I told him no. I asked him what he was waiting for. He said, "I don't want to make this final decision. I will just let my body run out of life, then I'll go."

I asked him how I could help. He said he really didn't need any help. He is doing this as fast as he can. He said, "It takes a long time with this type of illness. I don't want to be in a hurry." He says he just wants to feel safe and do it in his own time. He says to tell his wife to do the things she needs to do and don't be tied to his bed or situation. He has said everything he needed to, to the people in his life — now the struggle is with himself and his fears. He wants his wife to know that doing this alone — making the decision to go and sticking by it — is difficult. That's why he is going to leave it up to his body to break down and then when he knows there is no more hope, he will leave. He wants to tell people to come around when it is good for them. This is a struggle within himself. He is very focused on what he is doing, and that is why he appears to be so out of it. He says, "I'm scared, but I will get through it. But I hate it." Then he thanked me for communicating this to his wife.

I saw a young, dark-haired man. I got the name Charles or Charlie, and saw that he was waiting for Mark in the tunnel to walk him over to the other side. Mark's wife told me afterward that her deceased father's name was Charlie and that he had dark hair before it turned gray.

She called me three weeks later and asked me to communicate with Mark's soul one more time to see how things were going and if he needed anything from her. Here is the second communication with his soul:

4/6/95

When Mark was close to letting go, it scared him. He has met many souls on the other side who have come to reassure him of his new life. I see a grandfather in spirit who comes to him quite frequently. He knows he will go any day. It will just happen. He will be gone and he knows that. He wants to be in his body and communicating with us as much as possible. He feels a need to help everyone understand his plight. He is still frightened of the final breath. The final good-bye. He feels as long as he is talking, he is alive and well.

I asked his soul what does he need from his wife or others? His soul says he feels complete as far as others are concerned. He just needs to talk, to feel connected to life on this side of the veil. He is almost resolved about letting go. He says, "Just keep letting me do it my way. I am just about through my fear." He says to me, "Thanks for giving me the healings. They help me feel more clear-headed, which is ultimately what I need in order to leave."

The first time I saw Mark, his silver cord was still attached to the body. On the second visit it was almost completely severed, which indicated he would be going very soon and it would be sudden. The part that was still attached was by his heart. It was the love he had for his wife and family that kept him alive.

There was such a different feeling in him the second time compared to the first. He was not nearly as fearful and was much more peaceful. He had surrendered a lot, but felt caught between two worlds. The good news was that there were several deceased relatives and angels working with him. He told them he needed a little more time, and they weren't pushing him, just assisting in any way they could. They enjoyed him a great deal and told me they were happy for him because his struggle was almost over. One of the angels told me he was very thorough in his death process. A male relative (in spirit) told me Mark was just as stubborn as he was.

When I finished our last session, his soul was standing on the other side of the bed looking at everything. His soul's mind was very clear. He smiled and reassured me that everything was on schedule. He felt very peaceful. I heard him think Saturday, but he didn't say anything to me about it. Mark passed away two weeks later on a Saturday.

Souls That Leave, Souls That Linger

Souls have the choice to linger or to go quickly when they die. Sometimes the soul is out of the body before the death actually occurs; this happened with my mom's former boyfriend, Jerry. He died in a car accident, and when his soul visited me the next day, he told me he just went blank while driving the car and felt "whisked up" before the crash actually happened. He said he was in the light when he heard the crashing sound of the cars.

Another friend kept trying to go back into his body after he suffered a massive heart attack. Two angels standing by his body told his soul that he could not go back because his heart had exploded. He needed the angels' help because he did not accept his death and would have stayed even though it was his time to go.

The guides taught me that when a person's body dies in a violent manner, like a car or plane crash, the soul will leave the body before impact. They said that it is not necessary for us to experience the physical trauma involved in that kind of death. I assumed that was true in all cases, until a recent experience taught me differently. The following is a story of someone who put himself through a living hell because he did not want to die. (I want to warn you: the story is somewhat jarring.)

It started in class one night when the topic was death. I said I wanted to be present when an autopsy was being performed, simply because I was curious to see if the soul stays around the body. One of my students, Lisa, said she was a coroner and invited me to watch her work.

We tried several times to get together, but our schedules didn't mesh. One day I happened to be in one hospital she worked in and we got together rather spontaneously. She said she didn't have any bodies currently in the morgue, but she asked if I would I like to see her workplace and check out the vibes. She was curious about the possibility of ghosts.

The experience turned out quite surprising for both of us. During our drive to the morgue, Lisa told me about an autopsy she had recently performed on a man whose parachute hadn't opened. The force of the impact had broken his body into numerous pieces. It was quite a laborious task for her — she spent seven hours putting him back together before she could begin the autopsy. The insurance company had wanted to know if the man had died from the fall or if he had suffered a heart attack, which would affect how much insurance money his family received.

My mind was racing with questions. Why did he have to die like that? Did he have a feeling that morning that something might happen? Was he awake when he hit the ground, or had his soul already left his body? Was he still here or had he moved on to the other side? I assumed that his soul was not around at the time of impact (but that turned out to be wrong).

When we arrived at the morgue, I quickly scanned psychically to see if any ghosts were there, and I didn't see or sense any. We walked into the room where the autopsies were performed, and I began to sense weird little feelings coming from several little brown bags that were sitting on the table. I asked Lisa what were in the bags, and she told me that each bag contained a part of the parachuter's clothing. After about a minute, I started to feel the most intense feelings of terror I had ever felt in my life, and I had to leave the room.

After I told Lisa what I was feeling, she asked if I would like to check the vibes on his jumpsuit and parachute, which were stored in the freezer. As soon as she wheeled them through the door, I felt over-whelmed with terror. I could barely breathe. I suddenly felt as if I had become this man. I saw the entire experience through his eyes — and he was definitely conscious during the fall and the impact. I told her word for word what I was getting psychically. He was falling and falling, thinking about opening his chute. He remembered his instructor's method, but kept thinking he knew a better way. Because he insisted on doing it his way, he died. However, it didn't end there. The parachuter was so sure his way was the right way that he would not accept his death. His soul lingered at the accident while the police searched for four hours and picked up all the body parts they could find. His soul was sure that if the police got all the pieces and the coroner put him back together, he could get back into his body and go on with his life. I also got a clear picture that a significant body part was missing. His soul stayed at the accident site looking for it. His soul was dazed, believing that if he could find it, his body could definitely be put back together. I was curious, so I asked the coroner if there was a significant body part missing. She said there was, but she didn't comment on what it was, and I didn't ask.

As the coroner had suspected with other autopsies, this man's soul was present the entire time she was working on his body. He was repeatedly trying to influence her, to let her know where each body part belonged. He was obsessed with being put back together and did not want to accept his death at all.

I was truly amazed that he had such tunnel vision about his death. He seemed to think that if he didn't accept it, it meant he wasn't really dead. (I've met more than a few ghosts with the same problem.)

My psychic teacher told me that we are in death just as we are in life. The coroner told me that the parachuter's wife had described him as very stubborn, always insisting on doing things his way. I saw that his stubbornness not only caused his death, but caused it to be very terrifying for him as well.

I asked my spirit guides why this man had to have such a painful death. They said that the man's soul could have let go of his physical body at any time and would have avoided experiencing the fall and the impact. They also said that the man's soul would continue to deny this death and told me to talk to the soul daily until I could feel him let go of his earthly existence. Each day I said the man's name out loud and said that he was now out of the body and needed to accept his death and move on to the other side, to look for the white light and go into it. It was at least a month before I could feel the man's soul move to the other side. I was really glad his soul came to terms with his death, although my sense was that he was still very unhappy about it.

Suicide

When a soul chooses suicide it is usually a desperate attempt to stop feeling pain, but what is important to realize is that it only aggravates pain. In the suicide cases I have done readings on, 98 percent regretted it afterward. Some choose not to go to the other side, and they linger in limbo and watch our side for a body to inhabit —what we call possession. Others go on to the next dimension and are either aware of their suicides and depressed about it, or they are in "hospitals" slowly recovering if they destroyed their bodies with large amounts of drugs. Almost all wish they would have sought help here and had not done this to themselves or their families. They see how futile it was because they still have to recover from the pain they're in. And they also see what a great amount of pain they have created for their families.

Our emotional pain is not only in the body, it's also in the soul. So many professionals today treat depression as if it's just a chemical imbalance, which gives the message that it's simply a physical condition. Destroying the body will not destroy the pain. There may be a chemical imbalance, but deeper issues need to be addressed as well.

Several years ago a good friend who suffered from alcoholism and depression asked me for a psychic reading on his condition. The guides told him he was not to commit suicide in this lifetime. He had committed suicide in several past lives, never dealing with the hurt in his soul, and this was his last opportunity to work out the pain while in a body. The guides said we have to honor our bodies and our lives, and suicide is the exact opposite. Suicide is an act of destruction and is only rarely chosen by the soul as a lesson.

Those who commit suicide and do go to the other side eventually get on with their lives, but they may always have a feeling of unfinished business. Whatever they didn't want to deal with, or didn't know how to deal with, still must be taken care of — and chances are that's why they came here to begin with, to heal all that unresolved soul pain. The more lifetimes an individual commits suicide, the more intense the pain. I don't know what the limit is on how many bodies we can destroy before we are not allowed to have another one, but there is a limit. I have seen clients who feel driven to kill themselves, and I've seen in readings that they have committed suicide in a previous life and are here in part to help break that destructive cycle.

Someone I knew well killed himself a few years ago. About a year after his death, I asked my guides if it was possible for me to talk to his soul. I was able to see his soul on the other side, and he told me he deeply regretted his decision but was slowly getting on with his life. His unfinished earth life was a constant thorn in his side, and he just couldn't make peace with it. He was such a great guy when he was here; so many people loved him. It's really a shame that we hold the misconception that suicide is some kind of solution, because it's not.

I have communicated with many souls who have taken their lives, and I have met only two individuals who committed suicide and did not regret it. Both were young men in their early twenties. Everything in life was going their way. According to the families, there was no outward reason for committing suicide.

The first young man, Brian, told me he simply knew it was time to go. He knew all his life he would not be here past age twenty, and he had told his mother that since childhood. He always talked in terms of what his soul was here to accomplish. At age twenty he had a great job, a loving relationship, was well liked by everyone he knew, and he seemed happy most of the time. One day, for no apparent reason, he shot himself in the head and ended his life abruptly.

When his mother came for a healing about her grief, Brian's soul came into my office and handed me (in spirit) a white chrysanthemum to give to her. He asked me to please tell her that, although he missed everyone, things were going well and it was good to be Home. His mother told me that many times throughout his life, Brian would bring her a single white mum. She also told me that in spite of her grief she had always had a peaceful feeling about his death. We decided that that peaceful feeling must have been coming from him.

Todd, the other young man, was very much the same: He had everything going for him, and then one day he abruptly took his life. When his soul came to visit his father in the reading, his soul told us that suicide was one of the lessons he came here to experience. He wanted to know what it felt like because he was going to work with suicide victims on the other side.

Both examples are not typical of suicide stories, which is why I say 98 percent of them are a desperate — and useless — attempt to stop the pain.

The Soul's Memory

If it is the soul's choice to die, and if heaven is such a beautiful place, why don't we just let go when it's our time to die and gladly go there? Why do some of us fight death so hard? The reason is simple: At the time we are making plans for our life and our death, we are emotionally detached. Life isn't real to us yet; it is just a series of plans and experiences. After we begin this lifetime and start experiencing the plans, everything starts to change. Shortly after we're born, we start to forget about Home. We live in our bodies, and we grow up thinking earth is our home. We become emotionally involved with everything that goes on here. When our time on earth is over, when it's time to go back Home, it's usually hard for us to let go and move on to a place we don't remember. We don't want to leave everything we know and love.

The reason our memory of the other side is closed to us during our time on earth is because remembering would make life here too difficult (just as remembering our past lives would, also). We would always be Homesick. Our soul has lived many lifetimes and has acquired many friends and loved ones. Even though some of them may be here with us now, many more are living on the other side. Our lack of memory is actually a blessing. It would be difficult to focus if we came here with full knowledge of the other side and of all our past lives and all the souls we have interacted with throughout those lifetimes. We need to be focused on this lifetime to accomplish what we came to do. It's really that simple.

Remember when you graduated from high school? Throughout our schooling, almost all of us looked forward to finishing our senior year. When the day finally arrived, for some it was a welcome blessing and they never looked back after getting their diplomas. Others wanted to graduate but didn't want to leave friends and all that was familiar. Others had a very difficult time graduating and letting go of their high school experience.

That's exactly how our other graduation day — death — can be for our souls, depending on where we're at in our development. We may leave quickly and never look back, we may drag our feet a little bit, or we may prolong our graduation as long as possible. It's different for all of us and there are no hard rules as to how we're supposed to do it.

If we're an older soul, we've gone through the death process and returned Home many times. It doesn't take long for that soul to remember the reality of graduation. Younger souls, however, have had fewer death experiences and may take longer to let go and accept their physical deaths.

As a soul grows in knowledge from its various experiences, the cycle of life, death, and life after death becomes easier simply because it knows deep inside there's a divine purpose for it all.

Someone Else's Death Process

It can be very difficult to be patient and wait while someone we know is dying. People have often said to me, "Well, we're all here, we've all made our amends, we've told them they can go, but they're still hanging on. What is taking so long?" The fact that our loved ones take so long may have something to do with their living relatives, but those souls could be tying up other loose ends here or going to the other side to prepare homes while still connected to their bodies. Sometimes in our death process we go back and forth between worlds until we feel completely comfortable moving to the other side.

I have a good friend who is a funeral director, and he has shared with me many stories about death. He said there is one thing he hears all the time, and that is that people usually pass on when they are alone. Over and over relatives have told him that they stayed with their loved one around the clock, and the minute they left the room, the person died. Given what I have learned about the soul I would say it probably waits until everyone is gone so it can leave without feeling guilty and minimize the emotional impact of its loved ones.

Triangle

John, who had suffered a stroke while on the operating table for heart surgery, was doing very poorly. His family asked if I would channel healing to him in an effort to lessen his pain.

In the middle of one of our healing sessions, John was thrashing around and moaning. Suddenly his body became very still. I opened psychically and saw his soul standing alongside the bed. John's soul told me that when he was out of John's body John didn't feel the pain. When he was in, John did. His soul told me he preferred to be out of the body, but wasn't ready to die yet. He still had things to do. John's soul said he had some unresolved issues with his son that were being worked on at night when his son was sleeping. He said their souls were communicating and were slowly working things out. John's son was not conscious of their meetings, but was simply aware of dreams he was having about his relationship with his father.

One day John's daughter called me to the hospital because he was having difficulty breathing. When I got to the room, his soul was standing in the corner, with his deceased mother on one side of him and his deceased father on the other. John's soul introduced me to them and asked me to look inside John's body. I saw that John's lungs were filling with liquid, and his soul said it would be only a short time before his soul went to the other side.

I asked his soul if he needed anything special in order to go, and he said, "Just the triangle." I told John's soul that I didn't have a clue what that meant, and he said it didn't matter, he just needed the triangle and then he would let go. Throughout the day his soul traveled in and out of his body. Physically he was miserable. I kept trying to figure out what the triangle meant, but nothing came to me.

All day people were in and out of the room. It was as if everyone could sense that this was the day his soul had chosen to leave. Around 8:00 P.M. each of us, with the exception of his daughter, his girlfriend, and his favorite granddaughter, went in different directions to do something. I went to the cafeteria to get everyone something to drink. His other granddaughter went outside to have a cigarette. His son-in-law ran down to check something in his car. Everyone but the three people closest to him had left the room. John's daughter stood on one side of the bed, his girlfriend stood on the other side, and his granddaughter was at the end of the bed. There stood a triangle of the people he loved the most. He opened his eyes, for the first time in days, looked at each one of them, smiled, said good-bye, and died. Although his son was not part of the bedside triangle, he felt peaceful about his father's passing.

As I was returning to the room, one of the nurses told me John had just passed away. I went into the room and saw his soul moving through the tunnel with a parent on each arm. His soul looked so happy, so free. He turned around, winked at me, and said good-bye.

About thirty seconds later, eight angels came into the room. I told one angel that John's soul had already left, and she said she knew that. She said they didn't come for John's soul; they came for the family. She said they always come for the families, to comfort them and ease them in the process of their grief and loss. Right then John's daughter asked me if someone had just come into the room because it seemed to be brighter. There was an angel for every person in the room, each angel standing directly behind someone to bring comfort.

After the family had gathered around John and had said their good-byes, after the funeral home and a few close friends had been called, after everyone had seemed to calm down, the angels left the room. Since that night I've often thought how unfortunate it is that people who go through the loss of someone dear don't know about the angels at the time of death. They were very comforting for everyone in the room that night, even though most of the people hadn't known they were there.

We need to look at death not as the enemy, but as a special time for the soul. The soul's schooling on earth has been completed, and it is free to go home. For those of us remaining on earth, the separation is temporary. The soul that has left the earth plane is simply on the other side of the veil. It can see us, hear us. It still loves us. It is very much alive, even though it is no longer in its physical body here on earth.

There is no greater emotional pain than loss through death for those of us still living on this side of the veil. As long as we are human beings, we will continue to fear it, hate it, fight it, try to control it, and mourn it. It's our nature as human beings to fight against whatever would destroy the physical body, but death does not really destroy us. Our true self, our soul, never dies. We are eternal beings. That is our birthright as a creation of God.

This is what life on earth is really about: Our souls are on a journey to develop to our highest potential so that we can someday live in the seventh level of heaven. When we realize our perfection, we don't need to come back to earth and live lives over and over. Our earth schooling will be over and we will remain on the other side with all those we love.

Chapter 6

Life after Death:
Home Again

What most people believe to be the other side,
I consider home. We are all just working our way back.

— Sam DiPaola

F or some reason, I don't remember many specifics from my religious training about heaven or hell, other than heaven is where we go if we're *good* — and if we're *bad,* we go to hell. They both seemed scary to me. Heaven was the place I would have to go to someday, all by myself, if I was *good.* Otherwise . . . I'd have to go to that blazing inferno somewhere below us, or wherever hell was supposed to be, forever.

The question of whether I was being good or bad seemed to overshadow everything in my childhood. Would I ever get to heaven? What was it going to be like to meet God? Would He approve of me? Did He really sit on a throne with a long white beard in a faraway place and keep notes on my every thought or action? I wondered what people in heaven did all day. Did they have fun or just sit around and behave themselves? The whole idea of heaven and hell seemed so ominous that I didn't like thinking about it.

Fortunately, as I developed my psychic abilities and began seeing pictures of the other side, a lot of my preconceived ideas of heaven and hell fell away. The more I grew spiritually, the more I came to know God in a whole different light. I've described what I've seen so far of heaven. In this chapter I'd like to focus on what our new life is like after we die. Where do we live? What do we do all day? How does it all work? Can we still communicate with our loved ones on earth? What is the afterlife all about?

There is a thin veil that separates our world and the other side. It's like a wall where our third-dimensional reality ends and the reality of the higher levels opens, but most of us can't see the veil unless we've developed our psychic gifts. Those living in the next dimensions can see it, but it doesn't interfere with their hearing and seeing us.

When we die and our souls move to the other side, we are in a state of great transition. We are letting go of a way of life we have known for many years. We are saying good-bye to so much that is precious to us: our bodies, families, spouses or significant others, friends, pets, homes, cars, toys, hobbies, religious communities, careers or jobs, education, status in the community, dreams, goals, and earth.

Our souls go through several stages in this process. Our comfortable routine completely changes. We get used to functioning without our bodies. We no longer need to eat or sleep to keep ourselves going. We are not governed by the same laws as when we were in our bodies. We live in a different energy. We are dropping our earth consciousness and are remembering ourselves as souls. We are getting reacquainted with Home. We have come Home to rest and relax from our latest incarnation. We take as much time as we need to heal and regroup.

This process is different for everyone. For old souls, souls who were created a long time ago and have lived many lifetimes, returning is easy. They are familiar with their surroundings and are comfortable with their new routines. Newer souls have a more difficult time letting go of their lives on earth. They are still in the process of learning what heaven is all about and don't have a strong memory of Home yet. Intermediate souls vacillate, knowing their latest lives were simply ways for their soul to advance, and yet struggling with the process of letting go, wanting their lives to have been more.

If you saw the movie *Defending Your Life* (with Albert Brooks and Meryl Streep), you are familiar with the concept of life review. It was about how each person reviews his or her life after death. I must say, Hollywood wasn't too far off on this one. Life review is a very important part of what we spend our time doing on the other side after each incarnation.

It's my understanding that first we watch our lives as if they were movies and then critique them, being as objective as possible. We are the ones who make the judgments, with guidance and support from our guides and the Elders. We record everything important in our Akashic records, for example, what we learned, the lessons we achieved, and what we came to earth to complete. Then we ask questions: Do we owe any amends? Are we holding any grudges? Were we responsible for our actions? Did we take care of business regarding relationships, work, and emotional, mental, and physical health, or do we have some unfinished business we need to take care of in another life? The plusses and minuses of each important experience are recorded.

This isn't something we do in a day; it takes place over a long period of time, and only after we have healed enough to be objective. As the movie showed, we do have help. Our guides or the Elders work with us, recording everything to help us see how much we have grown. As I said in chapter 4, we go to our Akashic records to draw up plans for each new life, and this is the information we base our planning on.

Life on the other side is very active. We do not get angel wings upon arrival, as some people think. We continue to be who we were when we were on earth, but our lives are freer and we are not governed by the same restrictions. We live in homes, we have lives, relationships, and work if we choose them. I have seen souls golfing, fishing, playing team sports, painting, writing books and music, working on experiments, talking politics, and studying medicine. We still continue to learn and grow on the other side. Our souls never stop evolving, and yet, if a soul wants to take a break and just be for a while, it can do that also.

About ten years ago I did a reading for a woman who wanted to know why she had so many relationships and seemed so unlucky in love. She wondered if she would ever marry. The guides said she came into this life to study love. Her soul wanted to know every aspect of it because she wanted to be a teacher on the other side and teach about love. So far she had experienced a lot of pain around love, and it was equally important for her to experience the joy of love. They reassured her that marriage was coming and it would be a very satisfying one, and that her soul was very pleased with all she was learning and was looking forward to returning Home to teach.

The Nether Worlds

Limbo

Limbo is halfway between our world and the other side. It's a creepy place, one I wouldn't want to stay in. It's filled with souls who don't want to move on to heaven for one reason or another. The main reason is they're afraid they'll be sent to hell. They just look for bodies to inhabit (possession) or people to scare. They communicate with people through Ouija boards or automatic writing. They can easily convince people that they are a loved one from the world beyond simply by being with people for a few days and listening to them talk.

I strongly suggest that if you are depressed, lonely, have recently lost a loved one, or are an alcoholic or a drug addict, you stay away from Ouija boards and automatic writing. The souls in limbo are immature and derive pleasure from frightening people. You can ask the universe at any time to protect you from souls that are not on a positive path and it will be done, but just for that extra measure of protection, stay away from Ouija boards and automatic writing until you know what you're doing.

Hell

Because we've talked about life after death and about heaven, we better take a look at hell. Unfortunately, I don't know much about it. The guides told me there is a community on the other side similar to a hell, but they made it very clear that God did not create it. Our souls did. They created it out of a need to be punished. They said that some people are determined to go to hell when they die, so their souls live in that community. I have no idea what goes on there. I have never seen it in any readings nor have I met any souls that were condemned to hell.

According to the spirits, God would never create such a hellish place or send any of us to it. God is loving and forgiving. We are held accountable for our negative actions, so if we have harmed someone and have not made amends in some way, eventually we must. Sitting in a place of fire and brimstone won't help atone for the pain we have caused others.

I'm sorry I can't be more helpful for those of you who wish to know more about this hell-like community. Yes, there is a place where souls can go who feel the need to be sent to hell. No, God did not create this community. Our souls did out of a need to have such a place. Who sends our souls there? We do, based on our own guilt and shame. Can we leave? Of course we can. We've sent ourselves there and we are the ones who decide if and when we can leave. Then we begin our life review process just like everyone else.

Evil

Questions about hell inevitably lead to questions about evil. What is evil? Webster's defines it as morally bad or wrong, wicked. Harmful and injurious. We all have our own definitions of what we think it is. The though of evil conjures up mental images of a guy in a red suit, with horns and a pitch fork who slithers into our lives like a snake, unbeknownst to us, and takes us over, thereby causing us to become evil and do terrible things to people.

Many of you will probably be surprised by this, but according to the angels that work with me, evil is an experience we all go through and every soul experiences being evil, to some degree or another, during at least one of their lifetimes. If you can take the emotional charge out of that statement and simply look at being evil as another experience here on Earth, you will be able to understand this whole idea.

The guides also said that everything has two sides to it. In order to reach that state of perfection we are all striving for, we need to experience all sides of every experience. We don't become good, moral people by simply being good all the time. Something inside of us knows not to do wrong — and we have gained that knowledge from past experiences we've already had.

There are numerous souls on the planet right now that are having evil experiences in this incarnation. They serve as reminders to those who have already been there not to go there again. For many of us the expression that fits best is *"Been there, done that."* People who are not doing evil things to themselves or others have already been there and know not to go there again. We all suffer consequences when we hurt another soul, whether those souls are human or animals, and we learn by these consequences. Jesus gave us the Golden Rule: *Do unto others as you would have them do unto you.* Many younger souls haven't learned yet that this applies to them as well, so they do harmful acts unto others, but it all balances out in the end, when they inevitably have to face the consequences of their acts.

Hearing about all the evil in the world reminds us of what we're capable of doing to each other and hopefully keeps us on track, moving always toward what is good in life, and staying away from evil. Eventually we will grow in consciousness so that evil will truly be an experience of the past that simply does not exist in our lives in any form whatsoever.

Common Questions and Answers about the Other Side

Recently a client came for a session wanting to communicate with her deceased husband. Patty was having difficulty not feeling connected to him as she always had. She had many questions to ask. I asked the guides if they would bring him to my office so we could speak with him. I was concerned because it had been only three months since his passing and, as I suspected, it was too early for him to come over to our side. His soul stood in a beautiful garden setting. He told me he was able to communicate with me, but he needed to stay on the other side. He was in his own grieving process; he missed his wife and his life quite a bit. We chatted for awhile. He told us of his new life and talked about old friends who had crossed over.

Patty asked him questions about life on the other side that I would like to share with you. I have changed the specific questions and answers and created a bit to make them more general.

Q. Will he be there when she dies?

A. In most cases our departed loved ones will not only be there, but will help us through our death processes and escort us through the tunnel to the other side.

Q. What does he look like without a body?

A. Souls generally look the same as they did in their most recent bodies or in their latest life, except that they're transparent. They don't have all the aids their bodies needed, such as glasses or canes. They look much younger and healthier.

Q. Will he ever appear to her while she is on earth?

A. Most of the time, our loved ones' souls want to appear to us more than anything. They want us to know they are okay. They are now made of a fine energy, and no density, that is very hard to see. Even if they do come through the veil and appear to us, it is unlikely we will see them, but not impossible.

Q. How soon will he come to visit her?

A. This answer varies with each soul. A lot depends on how prepared the soul was to die. If leaving was very emotional, the Elders may well advise waiting until it is less painful. This is why some people feel their departed loved one right away and others not for some time. Also, they could be standing right next to us and because their energy is so light and because we're still expecting them to look more dense, like their physical bodies did, we might look right past them. Patience is the key.

Q. Could he help make decisions about the family business and some of his possessions?

A. This is a common question in this kind of reading — who gets what, how money should be invested, where the missing insurance papers are, and so on. To the soul it generally doesn't matter anymore. The soul is involved in a new life and has left behind those kinds of decisions.

Q. What does he do all day?

A. Souls are not governed by time, so their time is spent differently than ours. They relax, take time to heal from their latest life. They visit with old friends, help new souls coming over, work, learn new things. They do whatever they feel inspired to do. They do what we do — just about anything they want!

Q. What does he think of his funeral?

A. Most souls attend their funerals and have some feelings about them, but it's such an individual event. Some souls don't care what happens to their physical bodies. They see the funeral as a ritual for the living so they don't always attend.

I have seen images of some souls sleeping through their funerals. When they finally wake up, they see their funerals viewed like a movie. Death from a drug overdose is a common reason for sleeping through the funeral.

When my mom's boyfriend, Jerry, passed away, I saw his soul at the funeral standing by the priest who was doing the eulogy. His soul listened very carefully to every word being said. Then when the priest started singing and dancing down the aisle to the song "When the Saints Go Marchin' In," his soul sang and danced along. He looked so happy that they picked that song. Later, at the luncheon held after the funeral, his soul came up to me and said, "It isn't fair that all this food is for my funeral and I don't get to eat any of it." (His passion in life was eating.) I wanted to tell everyone what he said because he had the greatest sense of humor, but I felt I had better keep it to myself.

Back to the questions.

Q. What does he think of the other side?

A. I have never heard a soul complain about life on the other side. Every soul says it's absolutely beautiful.

Q. What does he think of his medical treatment?

A. Most souls are detached from it by the time they are asked that question. Some regret they fought their deaths so hard and put themselves and their families through so much pain at the end. I have met an occasional soul who feels resentful about its treatment, but generally moves on from that rather quickly.

Q. Can he see me?

A. Yes, souls can see us clearly. The veil is very thin.

Q. Can he hear me if I talk to him?

A. Yes, souls can hear us. All you need to do is say their names out loud and they can hear whatever you want to say to them.

Q. Does he come every time I ask him to?

A. No, not necessarily. Souls have their lives going on and we need to respect that.

A story comes to mind related to the last question. About twenty years ago I was seeing a therapist who did not believe in my abilities. He told me several times that the voices I thought I heard did not exist. He said none of it was real and that I needed to accept that fact. One day I asked if he would like to have one of my spirit friends come into the room so that he could feel its presence. He said, "Sure, go ahead." Silently I asked my grandmother to please come and somehow show this guy that she really did exist. About twenty seconds later, there she was. She stood behind the therapist and put her hands on his shoulders.

He started squirming. He asked me if something was standing behind him. I told him my grandma was. He stood up and moved to another part of the room and asked me to tell her to leave.

My grandmother told me she didn't like this guy. She said he wasn't a nice man and he wouldn't be helpful to me. Then she told me not to call her like that because she was right in the middle of something and it was difficult to break away. Then she smiled at me and left the room. The therapist asked if she had left, but made no further comment about it. For me it was a good lesson in learning to respect the soul's life just as we would someone on this side.

Communicating with a Deceased Loved One

Many people have asked me if it is possible to communicate with a loved one who has passed away and, if so, how to do it. Loved ones usually try to get messages through to us to let us know how they are doing. They will communicate through psychics. They will try to appear to us. Sometimes they will come to us and project a smell that will remind us of them. Other times we will be sitting quietly or perhaps taking a walk we once enjoyed together, and we will intuitively know they are there with us. They also work through electricity — turning TVs and radios on and off, affecting lights, doorbells, phones. They seem to be able to manipulate energy — most likely because they're energy!

A few years ago I was channeling healings to a dear friend who was dying of cancer. The afternoon he died, I was sitting in my kitchen. All of a sudden a breeze blew the kitchen curtain and someone held my hands for a brief second. I heard a voice whisper, "Thank you." It all happened so fast I wondered if I had imagined it. About an hour later a mutual friend called to tell me he had died. The time of his death was moments before my experience.

Spirits or deceased loved ones don't all speak. Some think to us; their messages come through as thoughts. What can make it difficult for the medium is that the deceased's thoughts and the medium's thoughts sound exactly the same, so the medium has to learn how to distinguish between the two. They also communicate with us through images, pictures in our minds. We receive pictures, one at a time. Again, interpretation is the key.

When trying to communicate with deceased loved ones it is most important to have patience. Often they are just as anxious as we are to communicate with us, but the timing has to be right for all concerned. If there is someone you want to communicate with, here are some helpful tips:

1. The biggest obstacle will probably be your intellect, which will tell you that communicating with your loved one is impossible. It is not.

2. If you are obsessed with wanting to communicate with your departed, that will block you. Don't make it the most important thing in your life. You need to get on with your life, just as your loved one must.

3. Ask that you hear from them either through a sign or in a dream. Place a tablet by your bed for recording your dreams, and tell yourself when you go to bed to remember them. It takes some practice, but messages will start coming through if your deceased loved one is trying to communicate this way.

4. When little things happen, don't assume they are just coincidences. Keep notes of the odd little things that happen — but again, don't be obsessed. You may sense a familiar smell, or thoughts may run through your head almost as if the person is having a dialog with you. Little things do mean something. There are no coincidences.

5. Don't try to complicate the process. The messages usually come

through in simple forms. When my deceased grandfather would visit me, I would always smell either green tea or vanilla ice cream. These are things he loved. My grandma brings my sister a bouquet of flowers whenever she visits her. My sister doesn't see them, but she smells them and just has a knowingness that it's Grandma. When a former male friend would visit, I would get the word "princess" over and over in my head. It was what he used to call me. Usually our soul friends have very little to say. They just want us to know they're there and that they love us.

6. Look for a reputable psychic who can contact souls on the other side. Not all psychics can, so make sure they know how. Go to a psychic you are referred to by someone you know. If a psychic focuses on negativity, tries to scare you, tells you there is a curse on you and for a sum of money can get it removed, *get up and leave*. This person is not on a spiritual path and you don't need this person's advice. You are fragile enough if you are in a grieving process — don't let such as person prey on your vulnerability. If you are desperate to communicate with a loved one, please let a little time pass so you can be objective when receiving information.

Here's a word of caution about obsessing: It's not uncommon when we are in a state of deep grief to want to know or feel that our loved one is nearby. We can't stand the void we feel, and some will do just about anything to communicate with a departed loved one. My brother

Michael did several ghostbustings for Carol, who had lost her daughter. She desperately wanted to communicate with her. For several days she repeatedly asked her daughter to come to their home and talk to her.

Then she heard banging on the walls, footsteps on the stairs. She felt rushes of cold energy. It all became too much for her, and she called Michael. I went with him on two occasions, and each time saw the same thing: her daughter wasn't there, but several other young spirits were present. Each time Michael cleared the house and cautioned Carol not to call any more spirits. She was so determined to make contact with her daughter that Michael's visits to her house continued for quite some time.

The last time Michael and I went together, I asked my guides to please help us. They gave me an image of a door that was open to the spirit world. (I've heard other psychics refer to these doors as portals, from our world to the other side.) The guides said to ask the angels to please take the souls back to the other side. Many of the souls we saw seemed to be confused. An adult soul from limbo was leading them as if he were in charge of everyone.

Many psychics are reputable and loving. They have the best of intentions, which is to bring you the guidance you are seeking. Two very good mediums I'd like to mention have great reputations for communicating with deceased loved ones: George Anderson and James Van Praagh. I've never seen George Anderson, but have heard his work is phenomenal. Two books were written about his work: *We Don't Die* and *We Are Not Forgotten,* by J. Martin. I have seen, James Van Praagh numerous times on television, and I have the greatest respect for him.

His book, *Talking to Heaven,* was a bestseller for several weeks. He is a highly gifted man, with a waiting list of three years. He travels throughout the country doing seminars. *

People ask me why anyone would want to talk with a departed loved one. There are many reasons. For certain people, some kind of communication with their loved ones is important so they can put closure on the relationship. Others may need information to understand the person's death, especially if it was a difficult one or a suicide. Often a murder has been committed and there are few clues to solve it. Psychic contact has been effective in police work. And we all have a need of some kind to keep in touch with our loved ones, whether they're living or deceased. It's more intense for some than others. They need to know their deceased loved ones are doing okay so they can get on with their own lives.

Here are a few examples of clients who came to communicate with a loved one.

It's Never Too Late to Heal the Pain

George came to me to talk with his mother, who had passed away ten years earlier. He had cancer and didn't have long to live. George had a strained relationship with his mother when she was living. She was very religious, very strict with him, and had instilled a lot of guilt in him he still

---

* His business address is 7985 Santa Monica Blvd. Ste. 109-135, West Hollywood, CA 90046. He also has tapes and videos. His website is http://www.VanPraagh.com.

hadn't resolved. He said he wanted to make peace with her before he died.

I asked the spirits if they would get her soul for us, but at first she would not come into the room. She was crying. After five or ten minutes her soul came into the room and said she had tried communicating with her son many times through dreams, wanting to apologize and tell him she had been wrong. She was beside herself with grief and guilt. Her soul said that she taught him what she had been taught, thinking that was the right way. But after getting to heaven and doing some healing, she realized that most of what she had believed and had taught him was a lie. She asked for his forgiveness several times. He cried, she cried. A tremendous healing took place that afternoon.

Justice Would Be Served

A mother and one of her daughters came to me to communicate with another daughter who had died mysteriously in a fire. They suspected the girl's fiancé had set the fire, but no one could prove it.

I could see the daughter's soul as she came through the tunnel and into my office. Then her soul described in great detail how her fiancé had knocked her unconscious in a hotel room, had driven her body to the building she was found in, and had set it on fire. His name was on the insurance policy. The insurance company had not yet paid the money because the circumstances looked suspicious, but no one could find any substantial clues. Her mother kept asking for some kind of concrete evidence she could take to the police. Her daughter's soul replied that there wasn't any evidence, but that she shouldn't worry because justice would come on the anniversary of her body's death.

Her mother and sister were really frustrated. I was, too, but I have learned that you can't push a spirit any more than you can push most people. As my clients left, I asked the mother to let me know what happened. She came back a week after the anniversary of her daughter's death and told me her daughter's fiancé had committed suicide on the date of her death.

Her daughter's soul came into the room, and all she said was that everything would now be just fine. The fiancé was in heaven and would have to contend with her and what he had done. She said, "Tell my mom everything's finally okay."

It's common sense to want some kind of proof from a psychic that the soul being communicated with is indeed the right soul. I think it is important to ask the soul to give you some proof, but I want to caution you as well. I have done many readings for people who want to communicate with deceased loved ones. Sometimes the soul will give many pieces of identifying information so that my client will know without a doubt that this is the loved one. Other times the soul gives a message that is very meaningful to it, but the client finds it insignificant.

Recently I channeled a message to a young woman whose mother had committed suicide when my client was a baby. The mother's soul poured her heart out, explaining all her feelings about taking her life and not raising her daughter, and about how she felt toward the girl's father. The mother's soul went through a great deal emotionally as she tried to reassure my client that the mother's suicide had nothing to do with her. The mother's soul disclosed a lot about herself and felt good about being so honest. I could see that the soul had been tormented for a long time.

The daughter asked for specific proof that this was her mother's soul. The soul looked at me with a sense of desperation. She was discouraged that her daughter didn't remember the events she had mentioned. I don't know why some deceased souls can recall things so clearly and others can't. In this case the mother's reality was so different now, twenty-five years later, that she didn't view earth experiences with the same dramatic feelings that we do. They were occurrences to her like many others, lessons she and her daughter had learned from.

The daughter asked if her mother's soul knew she was a grandmother, and the soul's response was, "Of course I know I'm a grandmother." The daughter asked why her mother's soul hadn't mentioned it, and the soul said she didn't understand what she was supposed to do or say. She knew her daughter was upset, but didn't know what her expectations were. She cared, but it was not the same real-life drama it was for her daughter. She was far more objective about it and far less attached to it than her daughter was.

When we go to the other side, we go to a very different culture. There is a prevailing calmness over there. The day-to-day dramas don't exist as we know them. Souls on the other side aren't caught up in the daily struggles we are or in the deep need to survive. They realize they have survived, and they see life here as a series of experiences to learn from. They don't always cling to the memories the way we have a tendency to do. They experience everything in present tense. There are no clocks or calendars, no time as we think of it. Yes, souls on the other side do have memories; they remember some of their yesterdays, but they're not necessarily the ones we remember.

Many people make up a code word with their almost departed loved one, thinking that if and when they go to a medium, the code word will ensure they have the right person. Code words don't always work. Sometimes the soul cannot remember what the code word was. I think it's because the conscious body-mind came up with the code word and perhaps it wasn't important to the soul.

I have seen many souls bring through all kinds of pertinent information, and yet, when they can't remember the codes, their loved ones on this side don't believe it's them. I suggest that, if you are in a situation like this, you listen to the information intuitively. You'll know if this is your departed loved one or not. Don't be too rigid and decide that the meeting has to go a certain way. Your deceased loved one is living in a new place, a different reality. Your loved one has been through a tremendous transition and may not remember all the details you remember or would like your loved one to remember.

Finally, remember that departed loved ones may be having just as hard a time as we are accepting their deaths. It's very important to respect their process. Pulling on them too hard makes it harder for them to move on. If you are having a difficult time with the loss of a loved one, don't ask your loved one to comfort you. Seek out someone here who can help you. If your loved one is having a difficult time, perhaps it will do the same on the other side.

Life after physical death is truly a reunion back to our real life, our true existence. Just as our clothes cover our bodies, our bodies cover our souls. When our souls move out of our bodies and move on to the next dimension, they are free — free to see and know the truth about themselves, their lives, heaven, and God. Most are so glad to be Home that they don't want to think about anything else.

Our souls planned their lives, were born into families who helped them live those lives, and met up with all the people and experiences they chose to have for their highest good. They gained a lot of knowledge and hopefully grew by leaps and bounds. When they were done, they turned in their physical bodies and returned Home, looking forward to a long rest.

Chapter 7

God and the Still, Small Voice

God intended us to have dominion
over our lives, to be the captains of our souls.

— Emmet Fox

Throughout this book we've looked at what a soul is, what heaven is like, and all the levels both of heaven and of souls as they evolve. We've seen the planning that our souls go through getting ready to come to earth. We've seen when our souls enter our bodies, and what happens when a pregnancy appears to have gone wrong. We've looked at the reasons for our lives here on earth and the lessons our souls take on, including choosing families and reacquainting with friends and lovers from former lives. We've looked at the death process and what that means to our souls, and finally, we've looked at life on the other side, what our souls do in between lifetimes, and where our real Home is. Throughout the book I talked about the ultimate goal of all souls: to develop to their highest potential and live on level seven, where they all have the same reality and totally know their oneness with God and one another.

God

For many, the word God or the thought of God conjures up a lot of mixed feelings, some of them negative. Many see the word *God* and want to put this book down — they don't want to go one step closer to the God they were raised to believe in or refused to believe in because they were taught that God is a jealous, angry, punishing God who sits in heaven and keeps records of everything they do and say. Many people would rather keep themselves separate from this distant deity who has the power to make their lives miserable. Tornadoes, hurricanes, volcanoes, and ice storms are just a few things considered to be acts of God. Who in their right mind would turn to this God for comfort?

In my work as a healer I've discovered that many clients believe their illnesses or diseases came from God as some sort of punishment for the things they've done wrong in their lives. My students have asked me why God allows all the suffering in the world or why He doesn't do something to stop wars and famine and poverty. They wonder why He doesn't care enough about us to change the horrible things that go on.

The key to overcoming all the pain and suffering we go through, individually and collectively as a species, is to find and maintain a relationship with the real God. We need to keep digging, to go past the negativity we've been taught about God and find the truth about our Creator and His relationship to us.

Several years ago I asked my guides how our souls were created, and they gave me an image of a vast ball of glistening white energy with an alive, almost electric feel to it. I could feel a deep knowingness within it. As the image evolved, I saw minute pieces separate from the whole. My guides said that the white energy symbolized God and that each tiny particle was a soul. God took a piece of Himself and created each of our souls.

Separation from God

In the beginning of our creation souls stay close to the source on the other side, but as time passes and our minds begin to develop, we have a desire to move away from our source and begin our schooling on earth. Once we're born on earth and our physical bodies and minds develop, we start to believe that our intellects are more knowing than the internal voice that has been guiding us thus far, so we slowly begin to rely on our minds and resources more than our Creator. As time passes, many of us forget entirely what our source is and how we are connected to that source. Most of us here on earth are searching for something to fill an inner void that we're feeling, and we've come to believe that it will be filled by something outside of ourselves.

In the book *For the Love of God,* Stephen Levine says, "In all our strivings, there is a profound homesickness for God." I couldn't agree with him more. The emptiness we're feeling internally is our separation from God. I would like to share a personal story with you because I believe it will help you understand the pain around our disconnection from our source.

When I was pregnant with my son, I would talk to him several times throughout the day, and I would rub my stomach and tell him how special he was and how much I loved him. I would hug my tummy and send as much love as I could inside. I was nineteen and single, and I knew in my heart that the best thing to do for him was to place him for adoption. I took the time that I had with him seriously and felt it was really important to give him the best "beginning" possible. He heard my voice and knew me as his source, from the time of his conception throughout his development in my womb. I held onto him for as long as I could (I was six weeks overdue when he was finally born), but I knew I had to let him go so that he could begin his new journey here on earth.

My son laid in the nursery for three days before going to his new family. Nurses held him and fed him, but for this tiny little baby, who had only known one source, he must have felt a deep sense of loss. The safety inside the womb and the voice that nurtured and loved him unconditionally was gone. His parents were very happy to receive him and they showered him with as much love and gratitude as they could, but they were a different set of voices with different feelings than the ones he had come to know and rely on, and I can only imagine that within that little baby, there was a deep sense of loss and separation from his source.

This is how our souls continually feel about our source until we once again find that energy that created us and become reconnected with it. Since finding my son, I've made a conscious effort to fill that void inside of him from our *physical* separation — and that's what all of our souls are striving for, a *spiritual* reconnection with our source.

Our world is full of overweight, alcoholic, drug-addicted, gambling, sex-addicted, shopaholic souls who are searching so hard outside of themselves for something that will satisfy that Homesickness. We do just about everything we can think of to distract us from feeling that disconnection from our source — and the distractions aren't working. My guides told me that we all crave inspiration, and when we don't get it we reach for anything we can find to soothe ourselves — which is why we're such a heavily addicted society.

For us to find the happiness, peace, joy, freedom, and inspiration we crave, we have to change our negative beliefs about God. We need to let go of our old, outdated images and beliefs and get with the program! God is alive and well and loves each of us unconditionally. God is not the all-punishing, jealous male being in heaven who is planning our next life crisis. So many of us turn to the heavens when something awful happens and ask, "Why me? Why did You do this to me?" We believe that if a tornado hits our house rather than a neighbor's, or some other misfortune befalls us, it was God's choosing.

We have it all backward. The truth is that our souls choose difficult or "negative" experiences to learn from, and God is available to help us get through them. The loving source that created us is here for us twenty-four hours a day seven days a week to give us guidance and encouragement. It's not God's fault that the world is the mess it is! We were given the world as a place to develop ourselves to our highest potential — and we're the ones who created the mess. Unfortunately, we're also responsible for cleaning it up. The good news is that when we go to God and ask for help, either with our own lives or for the recovery of our planet, we get the answers we need.

So many people are at a loss regarding where to begin when starting a real relationship with God. The journey for each of us will be different, so I can't tell you what will work for you. But I can tell you how my relationship developed over the years.

My Journey to Find God

When I was a little girl, I used to ask God to make something happen to my dad so that he wouldn't come home anymore. I didn't want to feel afraid all the time. I asked Him to please break all the whiskey bottles in the world and break all the machines that people use to make whiskey with. I asked Him to help my younger brother not be so nervous, and I asked if I could be as pretty as my sister. None of those prayers were answered.

When I was older, I prayed that my fear of boys would go away. That my acne would clear up. That my inferiority complex would go away. I prayed that my thighs would get smaller and that I'd be skinny. I prayed that my shyness would disappear and that I'd have confidence like everyone else seemed to have. None of those prayers was answered.

When I started college, I prayed that my drinking wouldn't lead to alcoholism. I prayed that I would get straight As. I prayed that my psychic abilities would go away. I prayed that I wouldn't get pregnant. I prayed for Mr. Right. I prayed for my health problems to go away. I kept on praying for confidence. None of those prayers was answered.

When I hit bottom with alcoholism, I prayed for help. When I got pregnant, I prayed for direction. As my psychic abilities continued to become stronger, I prayed to use them wisely. Each time I had surgery to heal my physical problems, I asked God to be there with me and hold my hand. When the direction came to place my son for adoption, I prayed for the courage to do it. Those prayers *were* answered.

For a long time I struggled with what God's role was in all my suffering. Why hadn't He answered my childhood prayers? If He really loved me, and if He was all powerful, why couldn't He have pulled a few strings and made things a little easier?

I wondered if He was at the helm of all human suffering, as religion tends to say. Is it true that He tests us to see where our loyalties lay? When people die, is it really God deciding He wants them with Him? And I was confused about the God-Goddess issue. Was God a man or a woman? Some said He was a light, others said an energy, others said a being like us — weren't we created in His image?

When I was on my journey to the other side, my brother told me to find God. I looked around and felt God everywhere. I felt the word God as I breathed and walked. Everything I looked at seemed to resonate God, and yet there was no one being looking at me saying, "I'm God." The trees, birds, mountains, flowers, hillsides, rivers, and streams — *everything* was God and I wanted to understand it all.

I joined a twelve-step recovery program for my alcoholism and codependency issues. I took my sobriety very seriously because I never wanted to go back to the self-destructive life I had created for myself. The third step says that we turn over our lives and our will to the care of God, *as we understand God*. I had always talked to God, ever since I was a child, but I had never really felt like I understood God. I knew in my heart that if I wanted what the program had to offer me, I had to become serious about my spirituality. I couldn't sit on the fence and kind of have a relationship with God. It felt like now or never.

My childhood vision of God — a man with a long white beard sitting on a throne in heaven — needed some updating. I still had the belief that God was outside of me far away in heaven, and I couldn't comprehend how He could distinguish my voice from the millions that were praying every day. I wanted to know if I was important to Him. I wanted to understand how it all worked. I attended church regularly. I took classes and read books. I attended as many twelve-step meetings as I could. I was thirsty for knowledge of God, and the thirst seemed unquenchable. Every time I learned something new, I wanted more.

I talked to God throughout the day. I wrote to Him in my journal at night. I asked Him to reveal himself to me. Teach me, God, teach me all about You — that was my constant prayer. Meditation wasn't my strong suit. I would try, but my mind would wander. I took classes, but that didn't do much, either. I asked Him for help with that, too.

One day I was on my treadmill, and I closed my eyes so I would stop looking at the clock. I saw a light inside myself, like a pilot light where my belly button was. Hmm. I had heard people talk about God being within, so I asked the light if it was God, and the light got bigger and brighter, so big that it completely covered my body. There was a wonderful calm, a serenity, that came with the light. Once again I asked the light if it was God, and I heard a very calm voice within me say yes.

Whenever I got on my treadmill after that, I wouldn't turn on the

TV or the radio. I would focus on the light inside and would feel so peaceful when I was done exercising. I talked to the light. I received answers, not in my head, but from the center of the light. At some point I realized that the voice I was hearing in the light and my intuition were one and the same. Soon after that I realized that the voice was the still, small voice within that the Bible refers to.

As time passed my concept of God completely changed. I saw in meditation that the light was the beginning of me. The light at the core of my being was God, and I realized what the expression "I am God" meant. When I say "I am God," I am simply affirming that God is the core of me. God expresses through me. I *am* one with God. God is my beginning and my end. This is my foundation, my inner strength and knowingness.

As I continued to know God, I realized that the Creator is not male or female, but is a perfect balance of both. I've realized that the Divine Spirit within me never changes. My soul is the one that's in a constant state of change, and my body is simply the vehicle that aids my soul's growth.

The process of knowing and understanding God as I do certainly didn't happen overnight. Over the course of many years deeper understanding gradually came. I could take in only so much at one time. I would discover a new piece, live with it for awhile, and then go back on the spiritual road to discover more. Somewhere along the road, I found out that God wasn't the one creating all the pain in my life. I realized that my soul had chosen the experiences of growing up in an alcoholic home, being an alcoholic, being an unwed mother and not raising my son, having health problems, struggling with low self-worth, being in and out of dysfunctional relationships, and being in a career that was not the norm. My soul wanted to gain wisdom from each experience. God never stepped in and stopped me from learning lessons, but God did step in (when I asked) and helped me get through each of them.

When I really understood that it wasn't God creating the pain in my life, but instead those experiences were life lessons my soul chose, my prayers changed and my relationship with God continued to change and heal.

The Still, Small Voice

God never intended us to go through our life experiences all by ourselves. His intention has always been to give us guidance whenever we need it. Two things are required, though: We need to ask for the guidance (God doesn't interfere), and we need to quiet ourselves so we can hear that still, small voice within.

Back in the early 1980s I went through a difficult time physically and financially. I had four surgeries within two years, which meant major doctor and hospital bills, and I had also taken a big chunk of time off from work to recuperate from each operation. All my credit cards were maxed out, and bill collectors were calling. My attorney advised me to file for bankruptcy; my pride said no. My friends and family helped out financially whenever they could, but I needed some big solutions, not little Band-Aids. Every day I asked God to show me clearly what to do, but no answers came. I was so discouraged. I felt really let down and alone; I thought maybe money wasn't one of God's concerns.

I went to my minister and vented all my anger about God not responding to my prayers for help. Rev. Clark reminded me that God doesn't shout, He whispers. He said when we're asking for guidance, we need to quiet ourselves enough to hear the still, small voice within. This advice only made me angrier because I wanted God to shout the answers to me, to put the writing on the wall. The last thing I wanted to hear was that I needed to quiet myself. When I'm full of fear or anger, that's very difficult for me to do. I had to admit, though, that it was very valuable advice and I've never forgotten it.

I worked hard at calming my mind so that I could go into the silence and hear the guidance I was given, which was to file bankruptcy. My pride and ego weren't too thrilled with the answer, but I knew, when I *felt* the answer, that it was the right direction for me to take.

I was raised by a mother who lives by her intuition and taught her children to do the same, so that little voice inside wasn't foreign to me. One of my guides told me once to think of it as my inner walkie-talkie, with God on the other end — that image always puts a smile on my face.

When I read Shakti Gawain's book *Living in the Light,* I formed a clearer understanding of how the inner voice works in our lives. One of the images that came to mind as I read the book was of a huge clock that exists in the universe, one that divinely times everything. When we're on our right path and living by the guidance within, we always end up in the right place at the right time and there's a certain magic in the way our lives work. We run into people we want to see and not into the ones we don't. We apply for jobs at the right time, call our friends when they're home at the perfect moment for a conversation. We're led to the right doctors, teachers, churches, schools, neighborhoods. There is a universal flow that goes on all the time, divinely guided by God, and when we get on the spiritual path we ride that wave with all the guidance we need.

When we're "in the flow" we feel our oneness with God, and we hear or clearly sense the direction we need. We don't balk at the guidance we receive because we've learned that the source that created us is filled with love for us and wants life to be easy for us. God wants to direct us, to show us how to move effortlessly through even the most difficult problems.

I ask daily for God's guidance in my life. I ask for God's will to be shown to me, and I follow what feels natural or right to do. We've all been raised to believe our minds are superior and we should be guided by intellect and reason — but, in fact, we've gotten it backward. The mystics teach that we should get our inspiration and direction from our inner voice, and then go to our minds and ask how to carry out the guidance we've received.

There is such a peacefulness in living from the intuition that I would never want to go back to the old way. Living according to what my head tells me or what society dictates robs me of all the magic in life, all the so-called coincidences and synchronicity. They're all part of the divine flow in life that shows us God really does exist and that He plays an active role in our lives.

How do we get past all the voices in our heads and hear the gentle one in the center of ourselves? First I need to clarify what the inner voice sounds like. It doesn't sound like an actual voice; it is more like a knowingness, or a knowing of words. You *know* the words you just felt are the truth. It's like having a thought in your stomach that feels really right. I know that sounds odd, but it's difficult to put into words. To hear that voice, you need to stop focusing on your head. One of my students asked me how he could tell if the guidance was coming from his head or from the area of his stomach or heart, and I told him to pay attention to where the voice was. Was it a thought in his head or a knowingness inside his being? We need to pay attention to where the voices are coming from and to the quality of those voices. Sometimes fear, guilt, and shame will be the voices from within our bodies, and they can drown out our still, small voice. Does the answer feel like fear, guilt, or shame, or is it a straightforward, nonemotional, knowing answer? When God speaks to us, it isn't with fear or shame.

Begin by asking for guidance with the small things in your life. Something I do daily is to write down all the things I need to do that day and ask God to show me in what order I should do these things. If I have to go to the post office, the grocery store, the bank, make some phone calls, and write a column, I ask for direction for perfect timing. It may sound trivial, but when I follow my guidance, there's usually no one waiting in line at the post office when I get there and I run into a friend at the grocery store. I see something happen at the corner while waiting for the green light that inspires me and I write about it in my column. Everyone I want to talk to is home when I call, and the people I want to leave messages for aren't home. It happens every time — divine timing guided by the divine inner voice. There are days when I don't get clear guidance, and I've learned that on those days the timing doesn't matter. On the days when it does matter, life works like a charm.

When you feel confident that you can hear the inner voice and you've practiced on the little daily questions, then ask for guidance with the bigger things such as job change, relationship problems, parenting, health concerns, finances, and so on. You don't need to close your eyes when you use your treadmill or go to a secluded mountaintop to find and hear the God within you. We all find God in our own way. It doesn't matter if your way is different from mine or anyone else's. What does matter is that you work at developing a relationship with your new concept of the real God who is living within you and happens to love you so much that it will take you the rest of your life to comprehend it.

We aren't meant to continually suffer while we're in the process of developing ourselves to our highest potential. Yes, life on earth can be very challenging and there are days, weeks, even months when it seems like we never get a break. Just remember: Your soul chose this life experience, and it is probably for reasons you will never figure out consciously. You have your family and friends to help you through the challenges, and you also have a higher power to help you.

If you don't have a good relationship with God, I suggest that you start by telling Him you want to heal your old pain with Him and that you would like to know the *real* God. Daily, ask God to reveal Himself to you — and then watch Him work through others. See all the anonymous little miracles that take place in your life.

Developing a relationship with the source that created you is by far the most rewarding relationship you'll ever have. That's where real fulfillment and peacefulness comes from. God's message is always one of love, of loving ourselves and opening our hearts to others. By listening to God's still, small voice within, we are led to fulfill our dreams and our highest potential.

Afterword

My Love Poem to God

I have been too long in the wilderness
Your prodigal daughter
Wandering from heart to heart
Too confused to settle into my own
But finally, at last, there is nowhere else to go,
But to that inner sanctuary
Where you've waited for me all along.
How now to make amends for my long absence
How to seek the comfort of your embrace
And trust that it belongs to me
At least to say — I love you, God
And wait for your reply

— Marcie New

About the Author

Echo Bodine is a teacher, spiritual healer, and one of America's preeminent psychics, featured nationally on TV and in other media. Paramount Pictures solicited her services for the promotion of the movie *Ghost*. She had led workshops throughout the country, and is the author of *Hands that Heal* and *Passion to Heal*. She has an extensive practice of consulting and healing and is based in Minneapolis, Minnesota.

If you would like information on Echo's other books or meditation tapes you can write to her at:

Echo Bodine
P. O. Box 385321
Bloomington, MN 55438

Recommended Reading

FOREWORD

Bunick, Nick. *In God's Truth*. Hampton Roads Pub. Co., 1998.
Ingram, Julia and G. W. Hardin. *The Messengers*. Pocket Books, 1998.

INTRODUCTION

Bodine, Echo. *Hands That Heal*. ACS Publications, 1997.
Bodine, Echo. *Passion to Heal*. Nataraj Publishing, 1993.

CHAPTER 1: *The Soul*

Harner, Michael. *The Way of the Shaman*. HarperSanFrancisco, 1990.
Ingerman, Sandra. *Soul Retrieval*. HarperSanFrancisco, 1991.
Monroe, Robert. *Journeys Out of the Body*, Doubleday, 1987.
Monroe, Robert. *Far Journeys*. Doubleday, 1973.
Newton, Micharl. *Journey of the Souls: Case Studies*. Llewellyn Pub. 1994.

CHAPTER 2: *Heaven: The Other Side*

Montgomery, Ruth. *The World Beyond*. Fawcett Books 1985.
Van Praagh, James. *Talking to Heaven*. Wheeler Pub. 1998.

CHAPTER 3: *Birth: Going Back to School.*

Wambach, Helen. *Life before Life.* Bantam 1984.

CHAPTER 4: *Life: The School Called Earth*

Bodine, Echo. *Passion to Heal.* Nataraj 1993.
Bowman, Carol. *Children's Past Lives.* Bantam 1998.
Hall, Manly P. *Reincarnation: The Cycle of Necessity.*
   Philosophica 1978.
Sutphen, Dick. *You Were Born Again to Be Together.* Pocket
   Books 1987.
Sutphen, Dick. *Past Lives, Future Loves.* Pocket Books 1998.
Wambach, Helen. *Reliving Past Lives.* Harper Collins 1984.
Weiss, Brian L. *Many Masters, Many Lives.* Simon Schuster 1998.

CHAPTER 6: *Life after Death: Home Again*

Martin, Joel. *We Don't Die — George Anderson.* Berkeley 1989.
Martin, Joel. *We Are Not Forgotten (George Anderson).* Putnam
   1991.
Van Praagh, James. *Talking to Heaven.* Dutton 1998.

CHAPTER 7: *God and the Still, Small Voice*

Bunick, Nick. *In God's Truth.* Hampton Roads Publishing 1998.
Cady, Emilie H. *Lessons in Truth.* Unity Books 1995.
Carlson, Richard and Benjamin Shield, editors. *For the Love of
   God.* New World Library 1997.
Fox, Emmet. *Sermon on the Mount.* Random House 1994.
Gawain, Shakti. *Living in the Light.* New World Library 1998.

Ingram, Julia and G. W. Hardin. *The Messengers: A True Story of Angelic Presence and the Return to the Age of Miracles.* Pocket Books 1998.

Karst, Patricia. *God Made Easy.* Warner Books 1997.

Rodegast, Pat. *Emmanuel's Book I.* Bantam Books 1987.

Rodegast, Pat. *Emmanuel's Book II.* Bantam Books. 1997.

I f you enjoyed *Echoes of the Soul,* we recommend the following books and cassettes from New World Library.

The Art of True Healing by Israel Regardie. This book centers around a very powerful meditation exercise — called the Middle Pillar — through which one can stimulate body, mind, and spirit. Through this technique, readers will learn to focus energy in a variety of ways for improving their health, success, and ability to help others.

Creative Visualization by Shakti Gawain. The classic work (in print for twenty years, three million copies sold) that shows us how to use the power of our imagination to create what we want in life. Available on audio as well, in two formats: the complete book on tape, and selected meditations from the book.

Living in the Light: A Guide to Personal and Planetary Transformation (Revised) by Shakti Gawain, with Laurel King. A newly updated edition of the recognized classic on developing intuition and using it as a guide in living your life.

Living in the Light Workbook (Revised) by Shakti Gawain and Laurel King. Following up her bestseller *Living in the Light,* Shakti has created a workbook to help us apply these principles to our lives in very practical ways.

The Individual and the Nature of Mass Events by Jane Roberts. Extending the idea that we create our own reality, Seth explores the connection between personal beliefs and world events.

The Magical Approach by Jane Roberts. Seth discusses how we can live our lives spontaneously, creatively, and according to our own natural rhythms.

Maps to Ecstasy: A Healing Journey for the Untamed Spirit (Revised) by Gabrielle Roth, with John Loudon. A modern shaman shows us how to reconnect to the vital, energetic core of our being through dance, song, theater, writing, meditation, and ritual.

Miracles of Mind by Russell Targ and Jane Katra, Ph.D. In this inspiring exploration of the mind's power, pioneering physicist Russell Targ and spiritual healer Jane Katra explore how our mind's ability to transcend the limits of time and space is linked to our capacity for healing.

The Nature of Personal Reality by Jane Roberts. Seth explains how the conscious mind directs unconscious activity, and has at its command all the powers of the inner self.

The Path of Transformation: How Healing Ourselves Can Change the World by Shakti Gawain. Shakti gave us *Creative Visualization* in the '70s, *Living in the Light* in the '80s, and now *The Path of Transformation* for the '90s. Shakti's new bestseller delivers an inspiring and provocative message for the path of true transformation.

Seth Speaks by Jane Roberts. In this essential guide to conscious living, Seth clearly and powerfully articulates the concept that we create our own reality according to our beliefs.

The Seven Spiritual Laws of Success by Deepak Chopra. A practical guide to the fulfillment of your dreams. An international bestseller, and for a very good reason. Available on audio as well.

Simple Truths by Kent Nerburn. Clear and gentle guidance on the big issues in life. Elegant, profound, and inspiring.

NEW WORLD LIBRARY
publishes books and cassettes that inspire and challenge
us to improve the quality of our lives and the world.

Our books and tapes are available
in bookstores everywhere.
For a catolog of our complete library
of fine books and tapes, contact:

New World Library
14 Pamaron Way
Novato, CA 94949

Phone: (415) 884-2100
Fax: (415) 884-2199
Or call toll-free: (800) 972-6657
Catalog requests: Ext. 50
Ordering: Ext. 52

E-mail: escort@nwlib.com
Website: http://www.newworldlibrary.com